Wake Up Your Soul

MELISSA KAZAN

Copyright © 2023 by Melissa Kazan

ISBN: 978-3-9825745-0-9

Editor: Nuray Elcin
Cover & Layout: Simge Tunc
AI Visuals: Melissa Kazan & Simge Tunc
Visual Editor: Omur Kazan
Picture: Onur Erdem

CONTENTS

Without your belief and encouragement,
this book might have remained a hidden draft.
Thank you for being my North Star
during this chapter of my life.

If you asked for a sign from the Universe and stumbled upon this book, trust me, this is the sign you've been waiting for...

Because the time has come to Wake Up Your Soul!

Chapter I

Introduction To Spiritual Awakening

A Journey to Awakening: Unlocking the Divine Connection Within

In the vast and profound universe, where galaxies dance, and stars collide, there resides a force, a spiritual energy that connects us all. This complex yet omnipresent energy is the core of our existence and the bridge between the physical realm and the infinite divine. The "Wake Up Your Soul" journey begins within this cosmic dance, guiding you to your authentic essence and showing you the path to spiritual enlightenment.

This is not merely a book; it's a spiritual quest, a path to self-discovery, and a guide to unearthing the secrets within us all. It's a blend of science, philosophy, religion, spirituality, and personal experience that weaves together to form a comprehensive understanding of what it means to be human.

As we embark on this journey, we will delve into the fascinating world of quantum physics, where the boundaries between science and mysticism blur. We'll explore the compelling connections between our thoughts, emotions, and the physical world, revealing the true power of the mind. We'll cross over the landscapes of various religious views, understanding how they align with our spiritual quest and offer diverse paths to the same ultimate truth.

Interwoven throughout these pages, my story is one of triumph, heartache, self-discovery and enlightenment. It's a story reflecting the human condition, filled with struggles and celebrations, doubts and revelations. I share my most intimate moments with you, not as a preacher or a guru, but as a fellow traveler on this path, someone who has stumbled, risen, learned and grown.

In "Wake Up Your Soul," you will learn about the holistic view of consciousness and the subconscious mind, the synchronicity between heart and brain, the paramount importance of emotions, and the need for mindful consumption. You will discover how our deepest beliefs, even those formed in moments of pain or despair, shape our lives in deep and lasting ways.

You will be challenged, provoked, comforted and inspired. You will be asked to look inward and reflect on your beliefs, desires, fears and dreams. You will be guided to heal, forgive, love and grow.

But this book is more than just concepts and theories; it's a practical guide filled with exercises, reflections, insights that will help you apply these profound truths to your daily life. It's a call to action, a plea to wake up, break free from routine and complacency, embrace a life of purpose, passion and fulfillment.

There is greatness within you, a soul waiting to awaken, a spirit yearning to soar. "Wake Up Your Soul" is the key to unlocking that greatness, the guide to finding your way back to the source.

The universe is calling. Your soul is stirring. The path to enlightenment is before you. Are you ready to take the first step?

Welcome to "Wake Up Your Soul". Your journey begins here.

Important Note for the Reader

In the unfolding pages of this book, you may discover passages or concepts that recur, echoing a familiar theme. This is not by accident but a deliberate choice. In many teachings, repetition is regarded as the master of skill, a method to deepen understanding and foster genuine, internal change.

I want to reinforce their importance in our quest for self-discovery and soul awakening by revisiting and exploring specific ideas from various angles. These repetitions are like signposts on a winding road, guiding you closer to the essence of who you are and what you can become. Embrace them as you would a chorus in a beautiful song, knowing each refrain is a step closer to harmony with the universe and your true self.

"Walk with those seeking truth."

- Deepak Chopra

Embrace Your Journey to Transformation and Love

I wrote this book two years ago, completing it in two months during the pandemic. Then, something curious happened: I stopped. Something inexplicable held me back, diverting my attention to other matters. I even found myself frustrated and self-critical at times, questioning, "Am I procrastinating out of fear of failure?"

With reflection, I've come to understand that everything unfolds in its own time. It's now clear to me that this book was meant to be published at this precise moment, not two years ago. Perhaps the world wasn't ready for it then, and maybe neither was I. We often grow impatient, wanting things to happen immediately. Yet, had I released this book earlier, it may not be successful or reach its audience. Furthermore, the additional knowledge I've gained over these two years has added depth to the work, filling in gaps I had yet to recognize.

In life, as with this book, timing can be everything. What seems like a delay is a preparation for the right moment. Now, the time has come to share these insights, knowing that they are more complete and that the world is ready to receive them.

My journey towards awareness and awakening has been marked by numerous trials and tests, particularly in money and relationships. I have struggled with fears of rejection, a nagging sense of unworthiness of love, lingering paternal wounds, and a persistent mindset of scarcity. For a long time, I saw myself as a victim, believing that my path had already been determined and destined to be fraught with hardship.

I envied those who seemed happy, wealthy and fulfilling lives and compared my struggles to their success. I felt as if I had been brought into this world to suffer, to be punished. In my darker moments, I reached a grim conclusion: God/Allah did not love me. Otherwise, why would I be given a life filled with pain and struggle?

As my consciousness expanded and I learned to surrender, the impossible began manifesting in my life. Miracles unfolded one by one, transforming my outlook and affirming my connection with the divine. I realized that I was not a victim of my circumstances and fully embraced the understanding that God/Allah loves me. Reflecting on my journey, I'm grateful for all the experiences that have led me to where I am today. Through this book, my goal is to guide you to a place of certainty and connection, to reveal the truth that God's/Allah's love embraces us all.

If you've acquired this book, recognize it's a sign: the time has come to awaken. Your Soul has been patiently waiting, and now the journey begins. Prepare yourself, for nothing will remain as it was.

As you delve into the insights within these pages, you'll gain the tools to transform both your conscious and subconscious mind. Embrace this opportunity, knowing that you are worthy and deserving of the very best in life.

Quest for Clarity: Understanding Love, Faith and Life's Trials

Almost everyone has a big or small problem. Some are tested with their families, some with their possessions, some with their health... Sometimes trouble ends, and one says, "Oh! I'm relieved," but after three or five months, a new problem arises. There is a saying, "God/Allah tests those He loves," but will we ever see the light of day? Why does God/

Allah keep us drowning in trouble? Are we just here to get tested? Or are we the ones who bring problems into our lives? What if we completely misunderstood Spirituality, Religion and Life itself? What if when we die, we realize we have misinterpreted everything? Wouldn't we be too late then? This book is not about Religion, but from my point of view, we can't deny its effect on us. Most of the Population believes in a religion or at least in a Higher Power who created the Universe. Some lost faith in God/Allah or Religions because of terrible experiences they had in Life. They felt maybe at one point abandoned by God/Allah. But to wake up our Soul, we can't skip this topic. We have to get at Peace with God/Allah again as Humanity.

No matter your religious affiliation or even if you identify as a nonbeliever, I invite you to approach the sections of this book about religion with an open mind. Set aside preconceived notions or biases and attempt to grasp the underlying message. It's a time for unity and heightened awareness.

Different cultures and traditions refer to the Creator as God, Allah, Elohim, the Universe, etc. Since I was born into a Muslim family, I tend to use the term "Allah", but throughout this book, I will mention it as "God/Allah". Please substitute this with whatever term resonates with your belief system. Remember, all these different paths ultimately lead to the same divine source.

Unfortunately, many individuals follow beliefs or practices without critical examination, unaware that their understanding might be misguided. A lack of knowledge about how the divine system operates often leads them from one life challenge to another, resulting in rapid fatigue and exhaustion. This misunderstanding lies at the core of today's most pressing issues, such as depression, burnout syndrome, feelings of alienation, and a sense of inadequacy.

The saddest aspect is that numerous individuals believe they are happy while telling themselves an immense lie to avoid the harsh reality. I fell into this trap as well. At this point, I want to unfold a segment of my journey. You may discover certain aspects that resonate with your life or intersect with your experiences.

I consider myself fortunate to have found love and married at age 27 in Istanbul, Turkey. I sincerely believed that my husband was the love of my life and that we were destined to be together forever. Sadly, about seven years into our marriage, I was confronted with the painful reality that I had been mistaken. Our relationship faced two significant challenges.

The first was my ex-husband's struggle with bipolar disorder, and the second was an ongoing conflict between our families, which escalated to the point where they stopped communicating with one another. Together, these two issues created an immense strain on our relationship.

I often felt very lonely throughout the marriage because my family abandoned me. My mother blamed me at every opportunity that I was married to the wrong person, and I was fighting hard to prove that I was not. On the other hand, because my mother-in-law did not consider me worthy of her son, I was also fighting. I was very tired of trying to prove something to both sides. Unfortunately, I had not noticed this at the time. Only when I came out of this war, did I realize how tired I was over the years. I was trying not to let anyone, not even myself, notice my unhappiness. When someone said, "Are you okay? You seem to be in a bad mood", I would immediately get defensive instead of telling my problem. While saying, "I'm fine", I would also say, "Don't lie; you're not in a good mood." But I was too proud to admit that I had failed in my marriage and life. I was never the one to blame. Everyone was guilty, but not me. It was always accessible, blaming others more than myself.

After living in Istanbul for about four years, I couldn't stand it anymore and told my husband that I wanted to return to Germany (where I was born and raised), and we settled in Germany with a joint decision. My ex-husband had given up his job and all his lifestyle for me. Divorce was out of the question at that time. We had small arguments, of course, but there was no need for a divorce. I have to add that my relationship itself was not bad. We didn't fight or even sleep one night apart from each other. There was some harmony between us.

But as time passed, the nightmare began. My ex-husband had severe difficulty adapting to Germany because he had language problems. He did not apply to job postings. After all, he did not know the language, and his motivation decreased daily because he did not find a job. Thus, a vicious circle was formed. I was trying everything to motivate him. We signed up for sports together, and we became members of different associations so that we could create friendships. I was doing my best to adapt him to our new life, but he stayed home while I was at work. Day by day, he started to stay home more and more. He stopped taking his bipolar medication, and finally, there was a man I didn't know anymore. I felt guilty and helpless. I started to be unable to concentrate on my work. This situation began to affect my performance negatively seriously. I forgot my to-do's, for example. My reputation as Assistant to the CEO was starting to suffer, creating a massive opportunity for those in the workplace who didn't want me. Apart from this, only one income entering the house also created a problem. I covered all the house expenses by myself for about three years. During this time, my husband's bipolar illness was on the rise.

Let me explain briefly for those who do not know about bipolar disease. Due to the deficient production of a salt called lithium in the brain, an imbalance occurs in the person. After a certain period of depression, he experiences a normal process. After this, a manic period starts (mainly in Spring and Fall Time), that is, excessive self-confidence, spending money, not getting enough sleep and hyperactivity. Since this cycle is continuous, they unintentionally upset the people they live with. So, taking medication is essential to keep them in Balance.

I constantly tried to convince myself that I loved my husband at that time. Yes, I fell in love and married this man, but the situation had changed significantly in the last two years, and I ignored it. We were far from each other. While I was improving myself with seminars and courses, he preferred to sit on the couch and watch TV. He became increasingly asocial and did not work or earn money. He didn't even help with household anymore.

My nerves were frayed, and I had lost my respect for him. I used to say harsh words and regretted what I said. I started living with a man who was staying at home and getting increasingly disconnected from life and I was helpless. Our fights escalated. This was not my dream relationship. I was the man of the house and he was the woman. We were both unhappy, but because we were in a deep sleep, we were unaware of it and did not accept it. We were still lying outside and to ourselves. Divorce? It was out of the question. However, there was no love left emotionally.

Still, I couldn't imagine a Life without him. If I were asked then, I would have said, "Yes, I love my husband" and would not say a bad word about him. You ask why? Because saying bad words about him would mean justifying my mother. I could never allow this. My biggest problem and my struggle was not to justify my mother.

I realized this much later. I was resisting hearing from her, "Look, did you see? I've told you" and others saying, "Oh, Melissa has divorced, look, she failed in her marriage." I was way too proud to accept failure. But the war was already lost.

So, how many of us are in this situation? How many of us are or were in a relationship that no longer serves us? How many of us are trapped in an unhappy relationship just because the other person is maybe good? My husband was and still is a good person. He was a beautiful human being with a pure heart. He loved animals, was always kind to everyone, etc. But while I was constantly improving myself, he was coming from behind. That's why our perspectives on life started to mismatch. Despite this, I have struggled because I felt guilty about changing his life just because of me.

I also feared people judging me and saying, "Look, she brought her husband to Germany, then left him because he failed." Well, does he not have any responsibility for his own life? At this point, my biggest mistake was this: I took his duties on my shoulders without realizing it. Because I didn't want him to be upset, and in time, I became his "mother". Creation has given everyone a mind, and everyone is responsible for themselves. I never feel guilty about it anymore. My conscience is clear because I did everything I could. I even took out a large amount of credit on myself for him to start his own business. There was no effort that I didn't make to make him happy; I focused my life entirely on him. When I reflect back now, I see how exhausted I was. When I looked with this consciousness, was ours love? Or was it respect and habit? I don't know. I believe my husband was my soulmate, but now I know there is no such thing as a single soulmate. Despite everything, there was harmony between us, as I said. Not once did he raise his voice or insult me. So, are these reasons enough to continue? No, it is not.

While my ex-husband in Istanbul was my dream man, the man in Germany became a nightmare for me. He didn't do me any harm personally; the circumstances did all the damage, and this was reflected in our relationship. Now, you may ask, "If you loved him so much, why didn't you return to Istanbul?" However, returning to Istanbul was out of the question, because I had no future there. Over time, we both developed differently and started not to look at life the same way.

Because divorce is seen as a shame and failure in our families, and because of the fear of what people will say, we did not even think of getting a divorce. However, my journey with my beloved husband was over, and what I never thought of came true: we divorced. Looking back, I can see that God/Allah, the Universe, wanted it to end, and it was apparent. Even our lawyer said, "I have never seen such a fast divorce process in my professional life." Sometimes, if something is going to happen, God/Allah is binding your foresight at that moment. What I mean is that I wanted to talk to my husband before the court and stop the divorce, but I couldn't reach him. During the divorce phase, he was somewhere else staying and was not reachable, so we met at court directly. Sometimes, when I look back and think about that process, I wonder how we divorced. If you had asked me before, "Did you ever imagine that you would break up with your husband?" I would have said, "Never, never, never..." I couldn't imagine a life without him. I thought I couldn't even breathe without him and never be together with another man. But I'm neither dead nor breathless. It was the opposite. After the divorce, I could breathe again. I even wasn't aware that I didn't live. You get only awareness when you get out of the situation.

Sometimes, we don't see the reality and tell ourselves big lies during the problem. The process after the divorce was a huge nightmare, a separate issue, but because I managed to go through that pain, I could continue on the path of enlightenment, and I was reborn again. A whole new Melissa showed up that I hadn't met before. I traveled more in the following three years than I have ever traveled in my entire life; I was free. Now, I am grateful for everything that has happened. I believe God/Allah loved me so much that He allowed me to free myself from this relationship. If I were still married today, I would probably be depressed. Unfortunately, many people in my situation hold on to their marriage and believe that if they get divorced, the world will end. Especially the number of couples who did not fall in love but got married is relatively high. However, if someone has not experienced love, they have not lived fully. To attain the love of God/Allah, we must first share human love. And that's why "Love" is the most beautiful, most precious gift God/Allah has given us, as long as we know its value. So, this part of my Story was my most extensive awakening journey, which is why I told you.

> **"Out of suffering have emerged the strongest souls; the most massive characters are seared with scars."**
> **- Khalil Gibran**

Discovering Divine Connection: Bridging the Material and Spiritual Realms

Unfortunately, since childhood, we have taken over many beliefs from our parents, the Society and Environment we grew up in. Society has passed on the beliefs to us that are known to be true without realizing it, and we have made them our truths. The problem is that what we record in our subconscious, especially between the ages of 0-6, shapes our lives, and if we do not transform it, it will continue affecting our lives.

Especially the beliefs about Money, Power and Wealth. Why do you think there are fewer rich people than middle-class and poor people? Because most of us were told that Money is evil.

Unfortunately, most people are not even aware of it. I have heard the word subconscious mind many times since I first became interested in such topics in 2011. I did not understand how vital the subconscious mind is and how it can negatively affect my life since I did not come across someone who explained it simply that I could understand back then. Now, I feel fortunate to be in this higher awareness. And now it is your turn.

People are going through a period of enlightenment and awakening right now. Along with this, the number of Coaches in the field of personal development has also increased as some do their job very well. Unfortunately, the number of people who abuse it is also relatively high. Incorrect information given by erroneous or incomplete studies causes material and moral harm to people. I have worked with many people disappointed and hurt by false Coaches. Thankfully, they reached the truth with the work I presented. But those who could not achieve this truth may be lost in incorrect information; maybe they felt offended by life and God/Allah. They thought that affirmations didn't work and prayers were unheard.

If you are one of these people, then know that God/Allah heard you and brought this book your way because the time has come for you to reach the truth.

If you combine all the pieces and begin seeing the whole picture, your life will change. For this, it is essential that you realize both the spirituality and the material realm.

Sometimes, we perceive that we have to make a choice; either we get stuck in the material world, or we will connect with our souls and lose our minds in this endless infinity. Let me explain quickly what is meant by infinity. In a broader sense, infinity can refer to an unlimited or unbounded quantity, space, or time.

I had many highly spiritual Clients who were not grounded and were disconnected from the material world. They had significant struggles with Money and other Material topics. Feeling that they don't belong in this world. Maybe you feel the same? However, there is no such thing as one or the other. When you experience both together, you start to enjoy life. What would it be like to have both in life? Like abundance, wealth, love, and even spiritually conscious and awakened?

We've always been told, "You can't have everything simultaneously." As someone who has experienced the opposite, I want to say: "You can have everything at once!" Because God/Allah does not mention that He has set limits anywhere. Let me give here chronological examples from the three holy books.

Book of Jeremiah: "Call to me, and I will answer you and will tell you great and hidden things that you have not known." **(Jeremiah 33:3)**

The Bible says, "Ask, and it will be given to you; seek, and you will find; knock, and it will be opened to you. For everyone who asks receives, and the one who seeks finds, and to the one who knocks, it will be opened." **(Matthew 7:7-8:)**

And the Qur'an says, "When My servants ask you concerning Me, indeed I am near. I respond to the invocation of the supplicant when he calls upon Me." **(Surah Al-Baqarah 2:186)**

You can see that all of these verses encourage believers to call upon God/Allah in prayer, promising that He will respond to their invocations.

Also, all three holy books give the same messages about that and many other things, as shown in the following. So, only stupid ignorance allows people to fight about religions. Remember that the purpose of the 3 Prophets was to deliver God/Allah's words to the people. And there is so much wisdom if you start reading it in a pure way with goodwill.

There is no such thing as punishment if we follow the right path. Punishment in holy books often results from disobedience to divine laws, which protect ethics, living, and morals. Punishment can also be seen as a warning and a call to righteousness. So, we are the ones who are punishing ourselves by disregarding those warnings. And I will explain to you what I mean by that. How many of us get signs from the Universe that we must end something, be it a relationship, friendship, or job, and still choose to stick to that and make ourselves suffer? Or how many people get a warning through accidents, health issues, or other troubles that they have to change their lives to better ones? Now tell me, is this your destiny or your unconscious choice? You have to be aware that every thought we send out is coming back to us (whatever it is). This means that every action we take has its consequences, be it in a good or bad way. You get out of this duality of good and bad when you reach divine consciousness and connect to the source again. So, what does this connection concrete mean? It means understanding that this divine Power (God/Allah/Universe) is within us and closer to us than our jugular vein (**Surah Qaf 50:16**: "And We have already created man, and We know what his soul whispers to him, and We are closer to him than [his] jugular vein.")

Let me give here again some examples from the holy books:

Genesis 2:7: "Then the Lord formed a man from the dust of the ground and breathed into his nostrils the breath of life, and the man became a living being." This breath of life can be understood as God's direct involvement in creating the human soul.

1 Corinthians 6:17: "But the one who joins himself to the Lord is one spirit with Him." This illustrates the intimate spiritual connection between the human soul and the Divine.

Surah Al-Hijr 15:29: "So when I have proportioned him and breathed into him of My [created] soul, then fall down to him in prostration." This depicts the soul as having a divine origin.

Here, you can see that we are a part of this divine. But we got lost in this overwhelming world at some point. Now it's time to remember our true purpose in Life and wake up our Souls.

Let me explain more about this Connection: To be conscious of the oneness (getting out of duality like good/bad, right/wrong), means understanding and realizing that wherever you turn your head, everywhere and everything is the divine consciousness. We are connected through a higher consciousness network; some are aware of this and some are not. For example, when we meditate, we tap into that network and connect our consciousness with the divine. It is a download of energy and information. This is also the moment where most of the inspiration flows. The most significant ideas come from stillness and a meditative state.

Challenging Faith and Finding Connection Through Divine Guidance in Our World

Besides that beautiful connection, it is also said in the holy books that God/Allah will test us. Why is that? I always questioned that when I was a Teenager. Why are there rich and poor? And why are there starving children when rich people enjoy life and throw food away on the other side? What kind of God/Allah allows that? Why is there so much injustice? All these questions lead to doubt me in God/Allah.

Let me give you examples about the testing topic: In the Torah, it says, "And you shall remember the whole way that the Lord your God has led you these forty years in the wilderness, that He might humble you, testing you to know what was in your heart, whether you would keep His commandments or not." **(Deuteronomy 8:2)** Here, the Israelites' journey in the wilderness is described as a test to see if they would remain obedient to God's commandments. The Bible says, "Blessed is the man who remains steadfast under trial, for when he has stood the test he will receive the crown of life, which God has promised to those who love Him." **(James 1:12)** This passage in the New Testament speaks to the blessings that come from enduring trials and tests faithfully. The Qur'an says, "And We will surely test you with something of fear and hunger and a loss of wealth and lives and fruits, but give good tidings to the patient." **(Surah Al-Baqarah 2:155)**. This verse openly states that believers will be tested in various ways, encouraging patience in the face of these tests. So yes, there is told that we get tested by the divine, but He does not mention that it will be permanent and that there is a blessing afterward. So the test lasts until we learn our lesson...

In the context of religious teachings, the concept of divine testing is often interpreted as a way for individuals to grow spiritually and morally. It is seen as a means to cultivate virtues such as patience, empathy, and resilience and to clarify personal values and commitment to spiritual principles. The tests of life are not necessarily meant to be understood as punishments but as part of a bigger divine plan that humans may not fully comprehend.

The existence of inequality and suffering in the world, particularly in the rigid terms of wealth and poverty, has led many to question the nature of God/Allah and even to doubt His existence. Different religious traditions approach this problem in various ways. Some point to human free will, arguing that God/Allah has given humans the capacity to make choices, and thus, we are responsible for the suffering that results from greed, selfishness or lack of compassion. Others emphasize the mystery of God's/Allah's will, suggesting that we cannot fully understand the divine plan and must trust His wisdom.

When you understand the true nature of your soul and recognize that there are endless possibilities in life, you will find absolute freedom. At that moment, you'll truly connect with the divine.

True freedom is doing what you love, making money with joy, eliminating the negative emotions that bring you down, spending quality time with your loved ones, having a pleasant and loving relationship and much more.

But this hasn't be entirely taught to us, neither in school nor elsewhere. Only if you were lucky enough to have parents or teachers who were aware and wise who maybe taught you that. Most of us learned more limiting beliefs than positive ones. Those wrong and superstitious beliefs continue to be passed on to children without questioning, so society cannot fully develop. Rich gets more prosperous, and poor get poorer until you and I stop this loop by changing those limiting beliefs. And it is not only about money. I will come to that later. This went on from generation to generation.

Especially in religious communities, there is more "Reliance on God/Allah." Of course, we are all entrusted to Him, but what if He asks us, "Why didn't you use your mind and take precautions first?" Let's see what the holy books say about using our minds and wisdom. **Exodus 31:3-5** in the Torah says, "And I have filled him with the Spirit of God, in wisdom, in understanding, in knowledge, and all manner of workmanship." This passage talks about God giving wisdom and skill to the people building the Tabernacle. It highlights how important it is to have intelligence and ability. In the Bible, **Proverbs 3:13-14:** "Blessed is the one who finds wisdom, and the one who gets understanding, for the gain from her is better than gain from silver and her profit better than gold." The Book of Proverbs often emphasizes the importance of wisdom and understanding. The Qur'an **Surah Al-Baqarah 2:269** says: "He gives wisdom to whom He wills, and whoever has been given wisdom has certainly been given much good. And none will remember except those of understanding." What the religions tried to tell us and what we are experiencing now are two different situations, mainly because of misinterpretations made without knowledge and reasoning. This ignorance has cost thousands of lives in the history of humanity, like the Crusades (1095-1291), the Thirty Years' War (1618-1648), or the Lebanese Civil War (1975-1990).

And if we consider major conflicts where religion played a significant or central role, there have been dozens of such wars throughout history.

The misuse of religion in history, such as the wars I've mentioned, is an undeniable reality, leading to skepticism and disillusionment with religious institutions. Many argue that these conflicts were driven more by human ambitions, politics and misunderstanding than by religious traditions' teachings.

In school, during history class, we learned about those wars; we witnessed some present wars in the media. So, when the awareness is not that high, it is normal for people to question and judge religions. Because it caused more trouble than peace, but was it indeed the religion and the books itself, or more the ambitions of humanity to rule the world by using the weakness of humans towards God/Allah and their beliefs and create war?

The holy books do not support war but have a vision for peace and nonviolence. The Torah says in **Exodus 20:13**: "You shall not murder." And in the Bible in **Matthew 5:9**: "Blessed are the peacemakers, for they shall be called sons of God." In the Qur'an, it says in **Surah Al-Baqarah 2:256**: "There is no compulsion in religion..." means that no one can be forced to believe.

Despite to which religion or belief you belong, do you see any conflicts about the messages given? So, if we read the books without judgment or bias, we would be much further in Life. Those books gave us guidance to connect to ourselves and the divine. And we should start reading them like other spiritual books or personal development lectures.

So this is one of the awareness I wanted to give you to wake up your Soul. Because as you have read now, what we call the Soul is the divine within us.

And if we want to make the world a better place, it starts with changing ourselves with you and me.

Let's remember that each individual feeds the collective energy field with their thoughts and energy. In other words, whatever energy each of us puts into this field, that energy returns to us through society. What we have to do, then, is to nourish this collective energy field with positive thoughts and emotions. But I want to make clear that our duty is not to save the whole world or the country you live in. It is not about that. With small steps, we will first beautify our own lives, and then we will begin to illuminate our surroundings, just as the light illuminates the room. Sometimes, we take the world's weight on our shoulders without realizing it. But the divine has no such expectation from us. So, we have to remove ourselves from this role of the savior. Our task is to take responsibility, of course, but as soon as you tag yourself as a savior of the world in an unconscious way, it will start to feel like a burden, and you will have no joy or ease in life. Take me as an example.

I am writing this book to give you some guidance in your life. I do it with joy, and I am more than happy if I can touch your Soul. But I don't try to force you to do things or to start believing in God/Allah if you don't want to. This means I don't put

any pressure on myself. I serve in the best way I can and give the rest to the Universe as a task because it is not my task to save the world but to be the light for those who lost theirs.

The Inner Struggle: Balancing the Primitive Brain's Desire for Safety with the Soul's Quest for Divine Connection

Now, I want to get to the next topic, starting with a question. Why do people continue to be ignorant despite so much updated knowledge? Because our brain likes to hold on to the known and what it is used to, that keeps it alive. It's a safe and familiar area. Our primitive brain has only one goal: to survive. It doesn't care about your happiness or satisfaction. Our ancestors survived with the information they passed on to us, which is essential for our brains. The brain says, "If my ancestors survived with this information, I can go on like this and survive too." However, it is not your brain that seeks happiness, but your Soul.

So we have on the one side the Soul, which wants to reconnect with the divine, and on the other side, we have our brain, which resists this by trying to keep us in our habits and patterns to stay alive. Getting out of the comfort zone is always equal to danger to the primitive brain. It is like going out of the Cave. As I said, we got many of our beliefs, positive or negative, from our ancestors.

For example, some of our grandfathers and grandmothers experienced war or poverty. And they kept things for a very long time and treated their stuff with special care.

They were saving money for any bad days that could come one day. And they taught our parents to be very careful with money, which is not earned easily (just as an example). Because this is how they learned from their mothers and fathers, and since this teaching is more dominant in their subconscious, our parents forwarded that information and beliefs to us.

We must now understand that our brain tries to put us in specific patterns and keep us there. So when the person starts to get rid of these stereotypes or starts to question things which is a deeply rooted belief in society (for example, questioning Religion and God/Allah), carries the risk of either being excluded or judged by the family or community because they may not tolerate people who think differently. So, when you try to get out of this Matrix, you must know that not everyone might support you on this journey. For example, I lost more than half of my friends. My mother judged me a lot during that period, and now she is my biggest supporter because she saw how my life changed radically. This may sound scary to lose friends and family members. But believe me; it is so worth it. Because now I have new beautiful friends who feel like family. I met a lot of like-minded people, and I feel understood by them. I have their support no matter how big and wild my dreams are. Before that, I had friends in a victim role like me and always talked negatively about how things to get are impossible (happy relationships, getting wealthy, etc.). After my awareness, I could not breathe with those friends anymore, and it made me feel very negative after I met them for Coffee, etc. So, the more my awareness raised, the more I got apart from them. It was an automatic process that I didn't force. Then, there was also a time when I felt a lot lonely. So, the transformation phase has its beautiful parts and challenges, which is normal.

When you, for example, move to another country, you also mostly start from zero and build everything from scratch. So it is the same with that. Don't be afraid of losing friends because you are not losing anyone. Only the dynamics change and space has to be open to letting new high vibrational people into your life because you got one of them. The same attracts the same. It is all about the energy you send out.

So being judged by family and society should not discourage you. The reason for this judgment and ignorance is straightforward: humanity cannot easily give up the usual things they know as the truth, and if you question this conventional system, you will become a threat to society. My purpose here is not to demoralize you by saying that you might be realized as a threat to society, but you have to be aware that it is not possible to get out of the box without changing your life and your environment. And this scares most people to change. But at this point, starts a kind of inner rebellion of your Soul that wants to wake you up. And you may get into an inner conflict.

When you start questioning life, you might feel isolated or estranged, often from society or oneself. It encapsulates a sense of discontent or disconnection that might lead you to question conventional beliefs or feel out of place among those around you. This is the point where most people start searching. And maybe this is why you are reading this book right now. Because you are searching for answers. And I feel so honored to be a part of your journey to yourself.

*"There is only one good,
knowledge, and one evil,
ignorance."*
- Socrates

Destiny and Free Will: Exploring the Intersection of Divine Plan and Religious Wisdom

You must know that massive amounts of DNA records over thousands of years are stored in our cellular memory, that is, in our subconscious. It is impossible to delete or change it at all easily on your own. If we make ourselves conscious and learn the truth, then the old thoughts that our brain has and the behavior patterns it clings to will begin to transform and change. Everyone has a different responsibility here. If we want to change this conventional system of society, we must first change ourselves. For this, the most important thing is to realize and live our essence, our soul.

The two most widespread religions in the world, which make up more than 50% of the global population, are Christianity and Islam. Unfortunately, they are mainly transmitted to people based on fear and threats ("being punished by God/Allah and going to Hell if you don't follow the rules"), which drives people further and further away from the Truth of God/Allah. However, we should know that if we are a part of the divine, moving away from Him means moving away from ourselves. The more we get disconnected from ourselves and our souls, the more we live a limited life where we cannot discover our true potential.

Did you ever ask yourself, "Why are others living an extraordinary life and I am struggling?" Another question is, are other people's seemingly extraordinary lives unique, or is it just a mask worn against the outside?

This is one of the biggest mistakes ever made. You are comparing the lives of others to your own and deciding that your life is terrible. So, is this your destiny? And if there is such a thing as destiny, then according to whom, on what basis does this divine choose people and give some beautiful and others a compelling destiny? If it were destiny, wouldn't there be a great injustice here? And if your destiny is fixed, you won't be able to change your life no matter what you do. I'm sure many of you have asked these questions in time. So I did once.

So let's go again to the holy books and understand what is taught there about this destiny. Some believe there is a destiny. Some believe they have everything in their own hands. I can say that both are true. You might hear a beautiful saying: "You might have a plan, but so does the Universe."

Here are again some insights from the three religions:

Free Will vs. Divine Plan: Jewish tradition holds that people have free will to make choices but that God also has a plan for creation.

God's Sovereignty and Human Responsibility: Christian theology often balances the belief in God's sovereignty over all things with the conviction that human beings are morally responsible for their actions.

Destiny and Human Free Will: Islamic belief includes the concept of Qadr (Destiny) or divine preordainment, but it also teaches that humans are responsible for their choices.

It is time to step out of this fatalistic victim role and return to wisdom, knowledge, and the truth of the divine. And for this, we need to decode the messages given to us hundreds of years ago.

We need to understand the authentic messages of the religions so that we can live a life beyond miracles.

Beyond traditional religious texts, many philosophical, ethical, and spiritual teachings and traditions share similar messages with religious doctrines. Some of these universal messages include:

Love and Compassion: Many secular ethical systems emphasize the importance of love, compassion, empathy, and kindness towards others. Humanism, for example, encourages a focus on human values and understanding.

Moral Responsibility: Ideas about right and wrong, ethics and moral responsibility can be found in philosophical traditions like existentialism, Kantian ethics, and utilitarianism, which often emphasize individual autonomy and responsibility.

Wisdom and Understanding: Philosophical traditions such as Stoicism, Buddhism (which some consider more a philosophy than a religion), and Confucianism focus on wisdom, understanding, self-control, and living in accordance with nature or a balanced way.

Meditation and Mindfulness: Practices like yoga, meditation and mindfulness, often rooted in Eastern traditions but not exclusively religious, emphasize inner peace, self-awareness, and connection with the present moment.

Human Rights and Dignity: International human rights standards and many national constitutions reflect principles of human dignity, equality, freedom, and justice, resonating with teachings found in various religious traditions.

Personal Development and Self-Actualization: Various psychological theories, like Maslow's hierarchy of needs or Carl Rogers's person-centered therapy, focus on personal growth, self-acceptance, empathy, and realizing one's potential, aligning with many spiritual teachings.

So, my main message is not trying to convince you and make you believe in a religion, as this is your own free will. But every teaching is telling us the same.

And if you get united and start feeling the oneness and connection, you will experience a significant spiritual shift. However, all the knowledge of God/Allah is written in the most recent three holy books, but if you read, for example, the Bible or the Qur'an in the Bus, you would probably be judged or classified by others. But if you would read another book with similar teachings, it wouldn't be a problem. And this is what I mean with disconnected. We ask the Universe for help or do Manifestation. We connect to Angels and Spirits. And who did create the Universe, the Angels, the Spirits, me and you? Isn't there a higher divine source beyond all that? And how would it be when we directly get connected to this divinity? Most people have never understood this knowledge or accused those who try to understand it of being irreligious and committing sin. Well, now is the time to wake up. If you want to discover the essence and infinity within you, you are especially obliged to understand the deep knowledge given to you through religious and spiritual teachings. At this point, I want to share some more teachings:

Hinduism: Teaches concepts such as dharma (righteousness), karma (action and consequence) and ahimsa (non-violence).

Taoism: Living in harmony with the universe's way through balance, simplicity and contentment.

African Traditional Religions: Various indigenous beliefs across Africa often emphasize community, nature, ancestors and spiritual balance.

Native American Spirituality: Diverse spiritual practices across Native American cultures that often emphasize respect for nature, community and ancestral wisdom.

Sufism: A mystical Islamic tradition that emphasizes inner spirituality, love, harmony and the personal experience of the Divine.

I found all the answers in Islam. I discovered the truth in it. In the Qur'an, **Surah Al-Isra 17:14** says: "Read your record." So I did.

And today, I am more connected to the divine than ever. I see in everything the oneness and love. And only those who are experiencing this can understand what I truly mean by that - being fully in joy, love and feeling free more than ever. All the manifestation works now, finally. And I will tell you how. This book is not only about religion, but also about how to get to this authentic connection.

Chapter II

Universe & Religion & Science

From Ancient Beliefs to Modern Misinterpretations: The Quest for Divine Love in a World Divided by Religion

Throughout history, humanity has believed in the presence of a higher force. In ancient times, communities that viewed the sun as a fiery sphere believed in the existence of multiple Gods in the heavens.

As time progressed and through the teachings of various prophets and holy texts, many people transitioned to a belief in one singular God. Today, the major world religions encompassing these beliefs include Islam, Christianity and Judaism.

Of course, there are more religions than this and we know that the main common goal of religions is to respond to people's search and facilitate the path of enlightenment. So, what are you looking for? The search for the meaning of life? And perhaps most importantly, what awaits us after death? Nowadays, many people are into spirituality but less into Religion, although those also believe in a Creator. Many people do manifestation and ask from the Universe. But who is this Universe? And why should we follow a Religion when we have this Universe where we can request things?

You must understand that it is not about un-thinkingly following a Religion but more about ac-knowledging the wisdom and teachings in the holy books. True religion offers guidance and in-sight, steering people onto the right path and foster-ing an awareness of the divine and the concept of unity. They provide a vital shortcut to enlighten-ment, saving us from a lifetime of searching for the truth. The existence of multiple holy books can be seen as an answer to the changing conditions of the times. As humanity evolved, updates were provided through new prophets to ensure continued guidance along the right path.

Even here, there is a divine plan. If members of different religions knew that there were many common points in the holy books, their perspectives would change. The most important common issue is that God/Allah created us out of love. Jesus gave the news of the Arrival of Prophet Muhammad in the Bible and said that He would be the last one. However, self-seeking clergy chose to exclude this chapter from the Bible because they saw the new religion as a threat. Unfortunately, religions are used not only for good but also for manipulation. How can people achieve true love in a system based on control and power? God/Allah replies to this question with "Read!". You get your answers if you will read the holy books and try to understand them.

While surfing social media, I sometimes come across religious videos that mention Abraham, Moses and Jesus, but others never mention Muhammad more than Muslims. And this hurts me every time I see it.

Like all other prophets, he was cherished by the divine. How can we draw distinctions between them? If we were to understand all prophets without separation truly, it would eradicate hatred in this world, replacing them with only divine love. The negative associations some make with Islam stem from a misunderstanding of the religion itself and the rise of profound ignorance.

We must awaken from this state of ignorance and sleep. Each of us is responsible for ourselves, so when the time comes to face the divine, we won't be able to say, "My God, I did not know." The **Surah Muminun 23:115** clarifies this: "Did you think that we created you in vain and that you would not be returned to us?". This emphasizes that ignorance cannot be our excuse, especially in an era when knowledge is more accessible than ever before. Our access to information today surpasses our ancestors, thanks to the internet. The wisdom we seek is often just a click away, eliminating the need even to visit a library.

Religion is not something we can comprehend with our five senses. All the prophets wanted to shed light on us and show us the way to go beyond our minds, and all tried to convey divine love. However, as I mentioned above, this valuable information in the holy books, unfortunately, led to wars and evils over time. This was because it was easier to manipulate people with a God, promises of heaven, and threats of hell. Since all the people who have questioned these issues in the past have been punished, the general public does not dare to question religions because this question carries a significant risk of exclusion. Since no one wants to risk being excluded from society, they either question but do not share or accept the information as it is without understanding. Especially in the past, this was the case; now, it has begun to change a little.

Understanding religion means understanding the divine system and order. There is very ancient information in the holy books, and the best way to understand this divine system can be through really understanding and realizing what is written in those books. Unfortunately, most people did not buy and read these scriptures to understand them. That's precisely why malicious people translated what was written in the book as they wished, conveyed it to people as they understood it and added fear to hearts instead of love.

We prayed to a God we seek in the heavens and beyond, asked for forgiveness, and wished to go to heaven. So, is this why the scriptures came to us? Or did the divine system want to tell us about the order hidden in this universe?

There would be no wars if everyone was conscious of this issue and discovered their essence and limitlessness.

Recently, religion has become less associated with love, infinity and mercy, but more linked to ignorance, backwardness and fanaticism. People now often speak of spirituality and appealing to the Universe rather than to God/Allah. Spirituality has become a substitute for religion, allowing people to avoid the chaos within religious beliefs. This shift is likely due to bias against religion, with many seeking peace and harmony through spiritual rather than religious teachings. But what if we could combine both? People neglect religion because they are taught to live according to the religion handed down from their ancestors and that they should never question their faith. Questioning religion was perceived as questioning God/Allah, which was not an option. Deeply ingrained childhood teachings discourage us from daring to question, with fears of sin and hell keeping us in line. This has led some to seek the divine through spirituality instead. You may have been spared this struggle if you're not religious, but the connection between spirituality and religion offers an intriguing path to explore.

When I was taught to pray as a child, I was filled with questions. "To whom are we praying?" I would ask, only to be met with the simple response from my mother, "We pray to Allah." Yet, this answer led to more questions. "Who is this Allah, and where does He reside?" When I pressed further, the only

explanation I received was, "Allah created us and is watching us; we don't question Him."

But why did God/Allah create us? What is our purpose in this world? Why do wars rage, and why do the wealthy discard their food when children in other parts of the world starve? These were the questions that consumed me as a teenager. I found myself fighting with judgment and questioning the very nature of divine justice. The apparent inequities of the world confused me, and I couldn't understand why so much injustice was permitted or, more critically, why God/Allah would allow it to persist.

How could ruthless people live in prosperity and enjoy their lives while innocent people suffer? I had come to such a point that I had severe difficulty believing in God/Allah. Along with this, I was terrified that I would go to hell for questioning Him. It is not my family's fault here because they passed on to me as much as they learned from their parents. Unfortunately, at this point, we see a social vicious circle. Since many don't dare to question religion, they pass on what they have learned to new generations, and new generations continue to pass on what they have learned to other generations, and this chain goes on and on. What would it be like if we tried to understand the books as what they really meant?

If we understood what our religion was genuinely trying to tell us, then we would have understood that there is no injustice. Everything we experience is our creation, and with it, it would be possible for us to progress faster in life. If we reach this consciousness and understand that everything is created from our thoughts, we will have the chance to work on ourselves, transform our thoughts, and thus change our lives drastically. But as long as we do not understand this knowledge, we will continue to play the role of victim, remain stuck in questioning divine justice, and will not be able to go a mile in life. Thus, the endless vicious circles continue and we think it is destiny.

So, let's discover, by combining religion with science and knowledge, how to release our potential and wake up our Souls to increase our quality of life.

People have forgotten gratitude, love and compassion, drowned in anger, disappointment,  sadness and hatred, and continue to drown. How can a person discover their Soul and infinity when they have all these negative emotions inside?

To discover infinity, which means unlimited or unbounded quantity, space, or time, as I mentioned before, we must first transform the deep negative information and habits in our brain; only if we empty the glass can we transfer new knowledge and positive beliefs to ourselves.

Therefore, it is necessary to understand the complex relationship between the subconscious mind, brain, heart, mind and spiritual body. If we solve this, we will be able to live a much better quality and loving life, and most importantly, we will be able to progress more easily and cheerfully on the path of enlightenment.

Now the choice is yours. Do you want to continue playing the victim role? Or do you want to radically change your life, discover the infinite limitlessness, and live the magnificent life of your dreams?

Let's examine and comprehend the issues individually and process them into our consciousness. I have often mentioned the word infinity until now, writing that this infinity is within us, which we should discover. But how can infinity fit into our body and soul when even infinity is expanded throughout the universe? And how will we solve this infinity within us when even science has not solved the universe yet? As I mentioned, God/Allah says He blew His spirit to us and tells us He is closer to us than our jugular vein. In other words, we carry His infinity within us. We need to dig a little deeper to understand precisely what this means.

Let's start with the universe. Because if we understand the greatness of the universe, it will be easier to understand God/Allah and the infinity within ourselves.

"The cosmos is within us.
We are made of star stuff.
We are a way for the
universe to know itself."
- Carl Sagan

From Black Holes to Galactic Scale: Grasping the Unimaginable Dimensions of Our Cosmic Home

As you know, Earth is part of the solar system. The solar system is part of the Milky Way Galaxy and is our home in the universe, an enormous structure. It has a disk-shaped structure that is about 100,000 light-years in diameter. The galaxy contains a spherical halo of stars and globular clusters that extends further outward and it's embedded in a more extensive halo of dark matter, which still needs to be fully understood.

The mass of the Milky Way is estimated to be between 1.2 - 1.5 trillion times the mass of the Sun and contains hundreds of billions of stars and a significant amount of gas, dust and dark matter.

There is a black hole in the middle of the Milky Way Galaxy. This is not just a particular case of our galaxy; it has been detected that there is a black hole in the middle of all galaxies. According to 2008 NASA data, the black hole of the Milky Way is called Sagittarius A* and has a diameter of 24 million

kilometers and a mass of 4,1 million times the mass of the sun. In other words, when you put together 4,1 million Suns, you get the mass of this black hole, and bigger black holes have already been found.

To imagine the size of the black hole, let's look at the distance of our Earth from the Moon. Our Earth is 384,400 kilometers away from the Moon, and it would be possible to place an average of 30 more Earths between the Earth and the Moon. (Source: NASA Spaceplace)

Here is another example for you. Assuming half of Country Turkiye is the Milky Way Galaxy, the black hole in the middle would be the size of a grain of sand.

NASA has determined that there are at least 100 billion stars in the Milky Way Galaxy, like in other galaxies. There are an estimated 2 trillion galaxies in the observable universe. This means there are about 200 billion trillion stars in the observable universe.

Of course, these are estimated numbers by NASA as the number of galaxies and stars in the universe is a constantly evolving estimate as astronomers improve their telescopes and observational techniques.

How can we grasp that the universe is infinite when it is so difficult for us even to imagine the size of our own Solar System or our galaxy in our minds? It is challenging to perceive even those trillions of galaxies existing and how infinite and limitless the universe is. I mean, look at these numbers. These are beyond our capacity for imagination. That's why I want to explain this part in detail so we can understand more clearly how big this divine system is.

If we explain the size of the universe with another example, we can consider the speed of light. The speed of light is 300 thousand kilometers per second, the equivalent of light going around the Earth 7 times per second. It takes 8 minutes for light to attain Earth from the Sun. It takes 25 thousand light-years to reach the center of the Milky Way and 2.5 million light-years to reach the neighboring galaxy.

Even these numbers can hardly be perceived by our minds. This is why we must go beyond to discover our Soul and Infinity. In all three religions, the creation of the universe is depicted as a deliberate and orderly process carried out by a supreme, all-knowing being. While the specifics of the accounts differ, they all emphasize themes of purpose, order and divine wisdom and power. The creation narratives serve not only as explanations for the origin of the physical world but also as foundational expressions of theological and existential beliefs about the nature of God, humanity, and existence itself.

Exploring the Invisible: The Mysteries of the Higgs Field and Dark Matter & Dark Energy

So, let's continue now with something else: the Higgs Field. But before we start, why is it important to know about it in terms of returning to our essence? At this point, I don't want to confuse you by giving too much detail and going into deep physical explanations. But the more you know about these fascinating insights about the Universe, the more you get fascinated by the divine system, which is perfect in my eyes. So let me explain. The Higgs field is a fundamental quantum field of the universe responsible for giving particles mass.

Without mass, fundamental particles like quarks and electrons would not come together to form protons and neutrons. Without protons and neutrons, there would be no atoms (I will explain the atom in detail later).

Without atoms, there would be no molecules; without molecules, there would be no matter as we know it. The structures that make up the universe, such as stars, planets, galaxies, and even life, rely on the existence of atoms and the interactions between them. So, without the Higgs Field, all of this wouldn't exist.

But this is not all. The Higgs field is an energy field that permeates all of space. In other words, it is everywhere, also in a vacuum! Unlike other areas, such as electromagnetic fields, the Higgs field has a non-zero value everywhere, even in a vacuum. This

means that even in empty space, devoid of particles and energy, the Higgs field still exists and has value. This non-zero value in a vacuum allows the Higgs field to give particles mass. Particles interact with this field as they move through space, and the strength of this interaction determines their mass. If the Higgs field had zero value in a vacuum, particles wouldn't have mass and the universe as we know it wouldn't exist. The existence of the Higgs field is not something that was "created" at some point in time or that comes from somewhere; instead, it's a fundamental aspect of the universe that has always been there, as far as Science has discovered until now.

To put it another way, if we remove the gravitational and magnetic fields, only the Higgs Field remains. So, it is not possible in any way to eliminate the Higgs Field. (Source: CERN) It is there. So, there's an omnipresent energy field everywhere. And why am I telling you this? Just as the Higgs Field is everywhere, the divine (God/Allah) is everywhere. We are all somehow connected with this energy in the middle of it. Is this the collective energy field I was talking about before? And when I manifest, does this manifestation enter this field and get my reality after some time? While the idea of a universal connection or higher intelligence is compelling and influential in various spiritual and philosophical contexts, it is not a concept that has a basis in current scientific theories. Some have tried to connect quantum mechanics to spiritual or mystical ideas, suggesting that the non-local connections seen in phenomena like entanglement might imply a more profound interconnectedness in the universe. However, physicists often criticize these interpretations as misunderstandings or misrepresentations of science. So, although there is no direct connection between Science and Spirituality/Religion and no evidence of the Existence of God/Allah, however, Einstein once said:

"Science without religion is lame; religion without science is blind."

- Albert Einstein

I want to continue with the Quantum Theory that describes the behavior of matter and energy on the most minor scales - typically at the level of atoms and subatomic particles. One of these is saying that observation Changes the System. That means the act of measuring or observing a system changes it. Until you observe a particle, it exists in a superposition of all possible states. Once you measure it, it "collapses" into one specific state.

When I discovered this connection, it was a profound realization for me. In the past, I would always calculate my potential outcome. For instance, if I announced a workshop, I would immediately begin to count how many attendees I might have to achieve my goal, thinking, "It would be good to get at least ten attendees." Can you see how this relates to the earlier statement? When I begin to measure, my boundless potential gets reduced to one specific outcome - the one I'm focused on. But what if I announced my workshop without measuring? What various possibilities might then emerge? Maybe I would get hundreds of attendees instead of ten? Could we limit ourselves to more outcomes than we realize through this thinking?

My main aim is not to explain Quantum Physics deeply but to convey its divine order and connect all these theories with Spirituality.

For example, you may hear about the Quantum Entanglement. Quantum particles can become "entangled" with each other, meaning that the state of one particle is directly related to the state of another, no matter how far apart they are. If you change the state of one particle, the other will instantly change correspondingly, even if it's light-years away. This led Einstein to describe it as "spooky action at a distance." Perhaps this phenomenon explains how individuals can sense each other's emotions even from miles away, considering our bodies are made of atoms. How else might a mother, from hundreds or even thousands of miles away, intuitively know that her child is feeling sad?

You might think you bought a book about awakening your Soul and landed in quantum physics now, and before that, I started with Religion. And yes, maybe you are now a bit confused or may be excited - or both. But now grab a Coffee or Tea and read that part above again. Me too; I had to read these parts repeatedly to understand these dimensions. So I can feel you. But this is the point where I want to connect both for you. Because imagine when you connect knowledge of Science and Wisdom of Spirituality and Religion; what kind of Superhuman would you be? The biggest challenge here is how you understandably connect both to improve your life and connect to your Soul.

Returning to the miracles of the universe, there is another issue I would like to address here: Dark Matter, the mystery of which still needs to be fully resolved.

Looking at the night sky, you see the stars and darkness... This darkness is seen as emptiness/darkness in our eyes because it does not consist of any known matter. So, is this darkness filled with something or is it empty? Or is what we call "Nothingness" hidden here? If we focus on this void, we will see that there is more immateriality than matter. According to NASA data, the universe consists of only 5% matter (!); the rest is about 27% dark matter, and 68% dark energy. Dark energy is one of the most mysterious and intriguing concepts in modern cosmology; its nature remains largely unknown, and it is not known what it's made of. Here, I don't talk about the spiritual dark energy but the natural one which exists in the Universe.

So, what is the difference between dark matter and dark energy? While they are both invisible and thus "dark", they have very different effects on the universe, with dark matter acting through gravity to pull structures together and dark energy acting to push space itself apart. Isn't that mind-blowing? One is pulling matter together, and the other is pushing matter away. They share the "dark" label because they do not interact with electromagnetic forces, meaning they don't emit, absorb, or reflect light and thus remain invisible. So here I am asking myself, what else is exciting but we can not see with our eyes? For me, it is the divine system, God/Allah.

The biggest challenge for some people is to believe in something they can not see.

At this point, questions about the universe and creation are endless. For example, have galaxies always existed, or was it the Big Bang? If so, what was there before the BigBang?

The most curious questions are: "What is where the universe ends? Is there an ending at all? Is the universe infinite, limitless?" In our mind, everything has a beginning and an end. The mind cannot perceive the concept of infinity. That's why science will always continue to seek answers to this. This is purely a matter of human curiosity.

Bridging the Divine and the Material: The Intersection of Religion, Science and Human Existence

In the vast complexities of science, religion often finds its entrance, illuminating the divine structure of the universe that bypasses our limited human comprehension because there is such a tremendous divine universal system that our minds cannot perceive and cannot explain it with our "tiny" minds.

The main reason for the existence of religions is (according to my point of view) that God/Allah sent us guidance through prophets to tell us about the divine order and universe and our reason for existence. Many view the genesis of religions as guided paths laid down by a Higher Power, revealing the divine order, universal truths, and our very reason for being. Of course, the holy books also include other essential messages besides spirituality. If we try to comprehend the valuable information written in books, we can find the answer to everything we question about life. The number of miraculous scientific explanations during that time is unexplainable. And it is so great that it can't be a coincidence. Numerous believers, myself included, recognize that the sacred texts of Judaism, Christianity and Islam offer insights that resonate with contemporary scientific understanding. While interpretations vary and not everyone sees these connections, here are some examples from the Bible and the Qur'an that some see as reflecting scientific knowledge.

Earth's Shape in **Isaiah 40:22**: "He sits enthroned above the circle of the earth..." Some interpret this verse as a hint at the Earth's roundness.

Hydrological Cycle in **Ecclesiastes 1:7**: "All streams flow into the sea, yet the sea is never full. To the place the streams come from, there they return again." Some have seen this as a reference to the water cycle.

Mountains and Earth's Stability in **Surah An-Naba 78:6-7**: "Have We not made the earth as a bed, and the mountains as pegs?" Some interpret this as referencing how mountains stabilize the Earth's crust.

Expansion of the Universe in **Surah Adh-Dhariyat 51:47**: "And the heaven We constructed with strength, and indeed, We are [its] expander." Some have interpreted this verse as an indication of the expanding universe, a concept central to modern cosmology. The best part is that there are now scientists who openly express and support this.

The prophets conveyed to people things that were impossible to know back then.

Knowing this, how can one reject this precious information that the holy books tell us? I want to give a few more examples on this subject.

Surah Rahman 55:19-20 says: "He released the two seas, meeting [side by side]; Between them is a barrier [so] neither of them transgresses." These verses refer to the phenomenon where two bodies of water meet but do not mix, such as saltwater and freshwater.

For example, this happens where the Pacific and Atlantic Oceans meet; the two oceans cannot mix thoroughly. This is because the water density of the two oceans is different. At this point, a border between them is mentioned in the Qur'an.

Surah Anbiya 21:32 describes the ozone layer: "And We made the sky a protected ceiling, but they, from its signs, are turning away." This verse refers to the atmosphere, which protects life on Earth by blocking harmful radiation from the sun, regulating temperature, and maintaining the air's composition.

Examples could go on for pages. We see that the Qur'an (also like the Bible) shed light on science centuries ago. You have to know that the Islamic Golden Age, from the 8th to 14th century, was a period of remarkable scientific, technological, and cultural advancement. During this era, scholars in the Islamic world made essential contributions to various scientific fields, and their work laid the groundwork for many modern scientific disciplines. Here's an overview of the critical impact that Islamic science had, both during the Golden Age and on contemporary science:

- **Preservation of Ancient Knowledge:** Islamic scholars translated and preserved works of ancient Greek, Roman, Indian, and Persian scholars. Without their efforts, much of this ancient wisdom might have been lost.

- **Mathematics:** Like Trigonometry and Algebra. The word Algebra comes from the Persian mathematician Al-Khwarizmi. His works laid the foundation for the study of Algebra.

- **Medicine**: Al-Zahrawi is often considered the father of modern surgery, and his works were used as reference texts in Europe for over 500 years.

- **Astronomy**: Islamic astronomers significantly improved astronomical tables and instruments. The observatories in the Islamic world were some of the most advanced of their time.

- **Chemistry:** Jabir ibn Hayyan, considered one of the pioneers of early chemistry and alchemy, conducted experiments and investigations into various chemical processes, such as distillation and sublimation.

- **Optics**: Ibn al-Haytham's "Book of Optics" was a groundbreaking work that laid the foundations for the modern study of optics and the scientific method.

- **Geography and Cartography:** Islamic geographers and cartographers created some of the most accurate maps of the time, contributing to navigation and exploration.

- **Philosophy and Methodology:** The emphasis on reason, logic, and empirical observation contributed to the improvement of the scientific method.

Now, why am I telling you this when the topic of this book is "Wake Up Your Soul" and now I give you a history lesson? Maybe you think I start now promoting Islam and the Arabic World. But I only want to show you what kind of wisdom lies behind all this. And the more you know the truth, the more you start waking up. If you understand that you must connect Spirituality with the Material World, you can create beautiful things like in this Golden Age.

Did you also know, for example, that during that Golden Age, Baghdad (Iraq) was Home to the House of Wisdom, a renowned center of learning where scholars translated and studied Greek, Persian, and Indian texts? It was a hub for scientific, philosophical, and literary achievements. I was lucky enough to meet a beautiful Soul from Iraq who explained to me more deeply about his country's wisdom. Before that, I would never plan to go to Baghdad, mainly because of the bad Memories I watched in the Media about the War. But now I can't wait to explore this wisdom hidden in this city. When you especially watch some movies, you can realize that Arabic countries are always shown with camels and deserts, as if nothing else. We are somehow brainwashed. What a shame... Maybe this is why the command to "Read" (Ikra) in Islam and the emphasis on reading and seeking knowledge in other religious texts also carry profound significance. Like it is written in the Bible: **2 Timothy 3:16-17**: "All Scripture is breathed out by God and profitable for teaching, for reproof, for correction, and for training in righteousness, that the man of God may be complete, equipped for every good work." **Surah Al-'Alaq 96:1-5** in the Qur'an: "Read in the name of Allah who created - Created man from a clinging substance. Read, and Allah is the Most Generous - Who taught by the pen - Taught man that which he knew not." These commands emphasize the importance of reading, learning and seeking knowledge as acts of worship. It signifies the vital role of intellect and education in human development and spiritual growth. Because when we seek knowledge and truth, there can't be ignorance or fights anymore.

Let me tell you a little story here. When the first command of "Read" came to our Prophet, He said to Allah: "My Lord, I cannot read or write." However, what Allah here told is different. He meant to read and understand himself.

"The Qur'an represents the human," said the Prophet Muhammad during a conversation. This means that those who read the Qur'an with understanding are reading themselves.

In my eyes, where science ends, religion and spirituality begin, but here I mean true loving religion, which is far beyond what we have been told.

"Knowledge should be used to understand the articles of belief rather than accepting them on faith alone."
- Imam Al-Ghazali

Exploring the Atom's Role in the Fabric of the Universe: A Journey Into the Essence of Matter and Energy

In the first part, I tried to explain how big the universe is because the concept of infinity is hidden there. I also started to explain some theories in Quantum Physics. Now, we will focus on the smallest particle in the universe, the atom... If we can understand the atomic structure, realizing that everything consists of energy will be easier. All matter in the universe consists of atoms; understanding the atom's structure is crucial in the journey to the essence.

Suppose you have a sugar cube in your hand, and you cut it in half, then you cut that piece in half again; then you cut that little piece in half again. If you thought about going on like this, would it be possible for you to split this sugar cube in half forever? Is it possible to divide an item forever?

When we put a sugar cube under the microscope and look a million times closer, we can see that this sugar cube is made up of atomic particles. Based on this example, it is possible to understand that everything is made up of atoms. No matter what material we divide into the smallest part, the point we come to is the atomic part. Of course, Quantum Physics also explored the atomic particle, but I'll touch on that later.

There are more than a hundred different types of atoms. Each one is different in size, weight and how it bonds with other atoms. Various substances, such as solids and liquids, can be formed this way. These differences are because the atomic components of a plant, animal and human are different. For example, there are roughly 126 sextillions (means 21 zeros!) of atomic particles in a sugar cube. I will give you a crazy comparison that blew my mind as I found it: the number of atoms in a sugar cube is roughly the same order of magnitude as the number of stars in the observable universe!

Can you imagine how many atoms a human body has? In addition, to give you an imagination of the size of an atom, when you divide a sugar cube roughly 33 times, you will reach the size of an individual atom.

So, what makes up what we call an atom? The word "atom" results from the ancient Greek word "atomos", which means "indivisible" or "uncututtable". Early Greek philosophers, such as Leucippus and his student Democritus, who lived in the 5th century BCE, coined this term. In ancient times, when technology was not yet developed, people assumed that the atom was the smallest particle. Later, it was understood that the atom consists of a nucleus and contains a miniature universe within itself.

An atom is the fundament of a chemical element, and it's made up of three main types of subatomic particles:

Protons: These are positively charged particles that are found in the atom's nucleus (the center).

Neutrons: These particles have no charge (they are neutral) and are also found in the atom's nucleus.

Electrons: These are tiny, negatively charged particles that move around the nucleus in what are known as electron shells or energy levels.

Here's a simple way to picture it:

- The **nucleus** is like the atom's core or heart, containing protons and neutrons.

- The **electrons** are like tiny planets that orbit around the nucleus, similar to planets that orbit around the Sun in our Solar System.

You can imagine the scale of an atom by comparing the nucleus to the head of a match and the entire atomic cloud to a large structure like a stadium. While the actual scales might differ, this analogy emphasizes that most of the atom's volume is empty space, with the nucleus occupying a tiny central portion.

Just as the universe has vast dimensions that challenge our comprehension, the inner world of the atom reveals astonishingly small dimensions. Exploring these tiny spaces uncovers the fundamental properties of matter and the rules governing the behavior of the building blocks of our universe.

Everything in our universe, from galaxies to people to the air we breathe, is made of atoms. But atoms are not just balls with protons, neutrons and electrons.

Inside the protons and neutrons, scientists have discovered even tinier particles called "quarks". These quarks are some of the smallest building blocks we know of, and they're part of what's studied in the field of quantum physics. These quarks are described in Physics as point-like entities with no substructure, meaning that they are not thought to be made up of anything smaller or more fundamental.

So, while we often think of atoms as the basic units of matter, the story doesn't end there. A world of smaller particles makes up those atoms, showing that the universe is complex and intricate down to the minor scales we can explore.

Atoms are like tiny universes with vast spaces inside. The solid part, the nucleus, where protons and neutrons reside, takes up less than 0.0000000001% of the total volume. People often call the rest "empty space", but it's not empty. It's filled with a cloud of electrons, which are so tiny they don't have volume themselves. This "empty space" accounts for more than 99.9999999999% of the atom's volume.

Here's the unique part: the quarks inside the protons and neutrons contribute only a tiny fraction of the atom's total mass. Most of the mass comes from the energy that binds the quarks together. So, even though atoms seem solid, they are mostly made of energy and empty space. It's a mind-bending concept showing the microscopic world's incredible complexity and wonder.

To imagine this, think of all the people in the world. If you could squeeze out all the energy and leave only the actual mass, everything would fit into something as small as a sugar cube. It's a fascinating idea that shows how everything we see and touch is mostly energy, even though it feels solid and heavy.

As we are mostly made of energy, what does it mean? Is this energy our soul? Is our essence and the spirit God/Allah has given us hidden in this empty space? Let me give you a crazy theory of mine: If the holy books says that God/Allah blew His Light into us, and Quantum Physics says that we are made up of 99.9% energy, then can it not be that this Energy is part of the Divine? Of course, I'm the one claiming this, not science. Let's get answers to this.

"Nothing exists except atoms and empty space; everything else is opinion."
- Democritus

Awakening Within: Navigating the Intersection of Spirituality, Science and Self-Discovery

After what has been told so far, it is clear that all these insights are genuinely astonishing. It could be too much physics for you or confusing at some point. I am sorry for that. But to get to your essence, you have to understand these elements. And at this confusing point, spiritual and religious beliefs come into play where our minds struggle with this large amount of complex knowledge. Because of this complexity, many people don't go that deep and look for the meaning of life. Unfortunately, many people are stuck in their daily lives and think that's what life is all about. Going to work, earning money, caring for their family (which is beautiful), etc., but nothing more. We cannot do anything for those who want to stay asleep, but the divine system will send the necessary tests for them to awaken those as well. Something always goes wrong in these people's lives; they mave face big financial troubles or health issues for example. These are the kinds of events that come to wake us up. So, everyone gets the chance to explore their divinity within.

I don't believe that God/Allah only exists beyond the skies. He is within us, in our bodies. You

only need to look in the mirror. Imam Ali once said, "You think you are a small entity, but within you is enfolded the entire Universe." This saying can be understood as expressing the idea that within each human being lies the potential for understanding and connecting with the Divine. It's a concept found in various mystical traditions, including Sufism within Islam, emphasizing the inner journey of spiritual realization. The most challenging thing in life is to understand the hidden mystery inside yourself and use it. Simply knowing about it doesn't change anything in your life. But when you begin to implement what you know, everything starts to change.

There is a spiritual movement in society at this time, and much information is being shared on the market. Those who set out on a path of self-discovery may unknowingly believe false information as truth and follow a wrong path. For example, if you only do energy work and never involve the subconscious

mind, your life will not change permanently. You may take energy sessions like medicine, but some situations keep repeating themselves. When you think your life has improved, you face another problem two months later. However, if you want a permanent solution that will last a lifetime, you need to involve the primitive brain and the subconscious mind in the process. We will come back to this in the following chapters. But I want to emphasize that I am not saying that energy work is useless.

On the contrary, I'm talking about how we can get great results involving the subconscious mind. Otherwise, something will always be missing. And many people get frustrated with the kind of misinformation I'm talking about and become wholly disillusioned with it. Which is a pity, as there is so much wisdom in spirituality and religion. The challenge is to find and change their lives with correct or complete methods. I'm saying this as someone whose life has changed completely thanks to this wisdom.

Here are some suggestions on how you can raise awareness in spiritual seeking:

1.) Listen to people with different points of view without judgment; look at what they share and learn about the subject they are discussing. If you don't understand what's been told, don't make that person's (perhaps wrong) information your truth because so many people are following this person.

2.) There is a lot of energy work being done in the market; be very careful because as long as you don't know who is transferring energy to you and how the energy you get will be like taking a drug that you don't know the effect on your body. The energy channel flowing here must be very clean. Otherwise, you can mess up your system without realizing it. If you have even 1% doubt, stay away.

3.) Many people serve people as life coaches or healers. Some are good, and some do it without having enough knowledge only to make money. For this reason, many people become victims of malpractice, losing unnecessary money and motivation. That's why you should definitely ask about the certificate and training of the person you are going to. The confident expert will not hesitate to show you their certificate and won't judge you. But if the person is getting angry, stay away. After all, you will hand over the most valuable thing to that person: yourself!

4.) Patience is crucial on this journey. Like in school, where we learn information little by little, the same gradual approach applies to understanding this wisdom. When we are ready, we'll be able to receive and understand the information that comes to us. We may get confused if we try to force the process. This could lead us to incorrect paths and methods, possibly even putting us in danger.

5.) You cannot achieve enlightenment without addressing and healing your traumas and underlying negative beliefs that hold you back. It's essential to mend the personal wounds in your life before diving into profound spiritual work. Many individuals desire instant enlightenment, which can only be accomplished by transforming these hidden barriers. Before you can soar to great heights, you must shed the burdens that weigh you down.

6.) Simply thinking positively won't be enough; you must also elevate your energy and vibrations to a higher level to transform your life. So, if there are negative records in your subconscious mind, think positively as much as you want, meditate, and try to manifest something into your life. Unfortunately, none of them will affect your life too much. The more you run away from this truth, the more you will postpone a life beyond magic.

7.) Understanding the whole picture is essential. More than simply focusing on spiritual aspects will be required; you must also consider the body. This includes grasping how our brain, heart, nervous system and overall body function.

8.) Recognizing what the subconscious is and how it transforms is equally essential. Once we've comprehended these aspects, we can proceed to the spiritual dimension and concentrate on that area. To absorb and apply this knowledge, we must increase our capacity, and we can achieve this by letting go of our inner negativity and making space for growth.

9.) Being grateful is essential. Even a simple sensation of gratitude can attract more positive things into your life. Constant complaining and expressing discontent demonstrate a lack of happiness with what we have. This attitude perpetuates a mindset of scarcity within us.

10.) To explore the infinity within ourselves, we must move beyond our five senses and escape our understanding of space and time. This is becau-

se our soul isn't limited to a physical location and the concept of time doesn't apply to it either. Time is only a reality within our senses. That's why being fully present in the moment is crucial. The present moment, such as when reading this book, is the only real and tangible thing. It's neither five minutes in the past nor five minutes in the future. So, how can we become so consumed by events from years ago or worry about future occurrences that haven't even happened yet?

11.) Explore spirituality, religion, and science as they collectively form a complete picture. We can only grasp the full context by understanding all three as interconnected parts of the same whole.

12.) Focus on changing yourself before attempting to change others. A common mistake in personal development is to immediately try to alter the people around us by imposing our newfound knowledge on them. This approach reveals a need for more understanding, as true wisdom comes from accepting things how they are. Only then will the people in our lives begin to transform. When you perceive yourself as flawless and blame others, you unintentionally drift away from your spiritual path. In this situation, hidden ego and arrogance can take over.

Chapter III

Self-Discovery & Authentic Living

Living Your Dreams by Breaking Free from Society's Constraints: Finding Your Path to Fulfillment and Truth

How many individuals can truly live the life they want? How many people can do the job they've always dreamed of? How many individuals unknowingly pursue dreams their parents forced upon them and didn't truly reflect their desires?

Perhaps our parents struggled with their jobs and worked hard to give us a better future. To meet their expectations, a child might abandon their dreams and start living out their parents' dreams instead. There are many other examples like this. Ultimately, are we living our authentic lives or just fulfilling expectations? Understanding this is crucial. That's why many people, particularly in middle age, start to wonder if they are living the life they dreamed of. Many people over forty make significant changes, like switching jobs, moving to new cities, or getting divorced. They do this because they realize they're not living their desired life. Though some are brave enough to take this step, I believe they're still in the minority. Many people don't make significant changes in their lives because of pressure from family, friends, and society. If you are in a similar situation, consider this question: "What advice would your 80-year-old self give you right now?" Time is the one thing you can't get back. Growing old and looking back with regret is one of the worst things that can happen. A group of journalists once visited a nursing home to ask the residents, "What is your greatest regret in life?" Surprisingly, the response is nearly concordant. The older adults express regret not for the things they did but for the things they wanted to do more of but never managed to accomplish. I'm asking you now. Is it worth delaying yourself and being in the same position as them? At what point in your life are you still putting things off or slowing yourself? People stuck in situations they don't like are likely to be unhappy. Think about those who hate their jobs. They often go to work in a bad mood because they can't pursue their dream career, and over time, their lives feel like a trap. They feel stuck in that job because they don't have another profession, and their mindset has trapped them in a situation that seems impossible to change. But it's time to change that. The solutions are all found in this book.

When we wake up our Soul and discover the infinity within us, we'll realize that we have unlimited options and will start to apply them in our lives. This process takes time and requires patience. Trying to rush through it won't get you to the goal any faster. However, it's worth knowing that if you take your steps calmly and without a hurry, you might be able to quicken the process.

Understanding the structure of the brain is crucial at this stage. Once you comprehend it, you'll see how to accelerate the process and proceed with strong and assured steps. Specifically, in the following chapters, I'll describe how the brain can improve in this regard.

Beyond the dreams our parents encourage us to pursue for our own good, there's also pressure from society and our surroundings. Statements like, "You will only gain respect from society, if you have a good education or a successful career", might have pressured you into living a life that doesn't truly align with what you want.

From a young age, many of us are taught that specific paths, such as obtaining a good education or building a successful career, are the primary means of gaining respect.

This message is reinforced within the family, at school, among friends, and through the media. Desires for a happy marriage or having children are also emphasized. Our subconscious may be influenced by these pressures in various aspects of life, even though we may not be fully aware of them. Of course, this doesn't apply to everyone. Some individuals are conscious and intentional about their lives, enjoying fulfilling relationships and pursuing their dream careers. There are many examples of people who have achieved this. Isn't that the direction we all ultimately want to head? Movies, TV shows and Videos on Social Media also play a significant role in shaping us. The information absorbed by our brain and subconscious mind can profoundly influence our lifestyle and thoughts. For example, if a movie portrays only successful individuals as admired in society, it can shape our understanding that recognition is tied to success.

Be mindful of what you watch and the messages it conveys. Consider love movies as another example. Each film portrays the struggles and challenges associated with love. While you might see it as just a way of storytelling, it's essential to recognize the underlying message about love being communicated to your subconscious. Suppose you accept that love involves conflict and difficulty and that finding true love is complicated. In that case, you may unconsciously create a reality where you attract challenging relationships. This happens because such beliefs shape your subconscious mind. And these beliefs aren't formed only through movies; your surrounding environment also contributes to shaping them.

"How many things have you held back from doing in your life because you were worried about what others would think?" Perhaps you always wanted to become a dancer, but societal pressures steered you towards a more "practical" career and you abandoned your passion for dance. Maybe you dreamed of traveling the world and exploring different cultures, but the expectations of settling down and having a family kept you from pursuing this adventure. Perhaps you had a talent for painting or writing but were discouraged from following those paths because they didn't align with your community's traditional definitions of success. Maybe you wanted to switch to a career in nonprofit work to help others but felt constrained by societal emphasis on high-paying jobs and status. Well, are you aware of how much you have given up on yourself in this life?

People who strictly stick to society's rules are like fish swimming in a bowl, confined to a limited existence. They might believe they are living their best lives, but in reality, they only exist. When someone starts to explore their spirituality and sees the unlimited potential within, they escape those limitations. It's like moving from a small fishbowl into the vast ocean. At that moment, life starts over again, and it feels like they are born anew.

We often hurt ourselves the most by not following our desires, worrying about what others will think, sticking to old ways of thinking, and accepting everything our family has taught us as entirely accurate. My goal here isn't to criticize parents but to emphasize that everyone should find their own truth.

Balancing Parental Respect and Personal Dreams: The Journey from Conformity to Authenticity

Honoring our parents is essential, and we must remember that we owe our existence to them. However, some people equate respecting their parents by fulfilling all their wishes and desires. They fear that following their own dreams and desires might disappoint their parents.

This fear has resulted in numerous unfulfilled dreams, symbolized by the metaphor of unfinished stories in cemeteries.

I, too, fell into the trap of sacrificing my happiness to fulfill the dreams and expectations of my parents, in my case, especially of my mother, as I had no connection to my father. At 19, unsure of my path, I started studying Business Economics to make my mother proud and graduated successfully. Her dreams for me were vivid and specific: a successful career in a managerial position, the perfect marriage, and two children (not just one, as she believed siblings were necessary). Unaware and without conscious realization, I followed this dream, believing it to be my own.

In truth, these desires were not mine but had been imprinted upon me since childhood. My mother consistently reinforced that achieving these goals would make her proud and happy. While she acted out of love, doing her best as a mother, her dreams for me overshadowed my authentic desires. Her love was genuine and built subconscious pressure on me, so I was left following a path that wasn't mine.

My mother's desire for me was caused by her experiences and fears. Having never pursued her education and being financially dependent on my father's income, she wished me a different life. Her protective instincts guided her to steer me toward independence and strength, which I am very thankful for today. At the same time, she was hoping I would marry a man on an equal level with me rather than a laborer like my father.

However, her well-intentioned guidance took on a more forceful nature. Whenever I introduced a boyfriend with lower qualifications than mine, she reacted strongly, pressuring me to end the relationship. Her tactics, which felt terrorizing at times, aimed to protect me but ended up sabotaging many of my relationships during my teenage years.

Though her intentions were rooted in love and concern, her actions unwittingly caused me heartache and confusion.

My teenage years were overshadowed by my mother's watchful eye and well-meaning but overbearing intentions. I found myself unable to enjoy this critical phase of self-discovery truly. Instead of seeking someone I might love, I began searching for someone my mother would approve of to avoid conflict with her.

Even though her actions challenged me, I recognize her good intentions and have long since forgiven her. Because I understood that she reflected her fears on me. I continue to love her, even when our desires for my life don't align, such as her wish for me to have children, a path I've never felt called to follow. Her deep care and desire to protect me have always been evident, and I appreciate that. But now I walk towards my own dreams and desires.

In life, one of the primary goals for a person should be to follow their own dreams. The challenge is to get out of the comfort zone once created. This conflict between wanting to achieve a goal and not being ready to leave the comfort zone can create a sensation of being caught or trapped.

Feeling stuck is one of the worst things you can do to yourself. But when you discover who you truly are, you can break free from this feeling and change your energy. And when your energy changes, staying in your comfort zone isn't an option anymore. Even if this seems impossible in some family situations, remember that everything is made of energy, so anything is possible in life.

If you start following your dream, you will realize that the whole divine system starts supporting you in a magical way that even you wouldn't believe it.

With success comes also mostly financial ease, which might attract considerable envy in society. Consequently, many people may un-intentionally sabotage their success and financial well-being to avoid this envy. Especially if there is a belief pattern such as "Successful people are always envied" in the subconscious, then the person may constantly sabotage himself without realizing it. For example, a person makes much money but spends it all to avoid standing out, so the money comes and goes quickly. In this way, the subconscious mind protects itself from possible envy. Of course, other belief patterns may also play a role here. For example, if a person's ancestors have always believed in a lack of money, this belief might be in the person's genes. Because of this, the person might unknowingly sabotage their success with money, feeling deep inside that they don't deserve to be wealthy. I will explain the role of our ancestors and genetic coding in depth in the next section, as it is one of the critical issues that we must understand.

But why such envy in society? Why does the community often pull down those who achieve success, wealth, and happiness instead of encouraging and promoting these accomplishments? However, wouldn't it be better to take this success as an example, support each other, and be happy together?

Unity consciousness comes into play here. If we discover the essence within us, God/Allah, and our infinity, we will all understand that we are part of the whole, should support each other, and want each other's happiness. Many individuals are unaware of endless possibilities and unity, as their limits and routines confine them. Therefore, people with a higher level of consciousness might face significant challenges in society because others may not understand them fully. However, this doesn't mean that community will necessarily make things difficult for you as your awareness grows. In contrast, as your consciousness grows, you'll reach a point where you have control rather than society controlling you. Once you've changed your subconscious thinking, you'll see that it was your subconscious that attracts even envy.

Let me give you an example. Suppose you have difficulty getting along with a person. It's as if one of you speaks Chinese, and the other speaks Spanish. But if you develop your consciousness, just like learning a language, you will be able to understand the other person, and you will be able to dominate the situation. You may approach that person from a different point of view and get a new harmony, or maybe that person will naturally disappear from your life because they no longer fit your level of consciousness.

Your energy and frequency will be so elevated that misunderstandings or negativity won't affect you. Nobody will be able to pull you down anymore. Recognizing your inner strength and ability means understanding that you don't depend on others. This doesn't mean you'll be alone. You'll connect with people who match your energy level. Focus on improving your energy, and you'll attract more

positive and enjoyable people into your life. For example, let's look at the animal kingdom. Have you ever seen lions befriend rabbits? Or that bears roam with elephants? I'll return to this topic later because you must understand the dynamics here.

Mirroring and Awakening: Observing Reflections from Realities in Our Spiritual Journey

In the spiritual community, the idea of mirroring is frequently discussed. Mirroring means that our energy and thoughts are reflected in us by our environment. However, there's a delicate balance to understand here, and I want to explain it carefully. Because I've seen many people get confused or manipulated by this without realizing it. And one of them was me. At one point, when you start getting a higher consciousness level, you begin to observe your surroundings without getting affected or triggered.

What do I mean here? When I raised my awareness, I started to see my friend's ego or sensed jealousy I wasn't aware of before. But I had problems distinguishing if it was an observation or if they were maybe mirroring something back to me. And I started to question myself like, "Is this my own Ego I see in them?" "Is there any jealousy of mine which I see there?" But honestly, this got overwhelming when I started looking for meaning in nearly every event in my life.

I was constantly asking myself, "What is this mirroring to me? What does this mean?" Eventually, I found that this constant searching was wearing me out. I even began to pull away from this spiritual journey, no longer finding joy in it. I became afraid that every step I took might carry some hidden sign from the universe, and I was gripped by the fear that ignoring these signs might cause me more pain and tests. I was torn between wanting to awaken spiritually and fearing the challenges that might come with it.

I placed too much trust in others who claim-ed to have all the answers on this spiritual path, often believing them without thinking for myself. For instance, if I shared an experience with them, they instantly asked, "What is this mirroring to you?" And I really couldn't hear it anymore.

I doubted my own Intuition. Eventually, I got tired of hearing this question and unthinkingly following their guidance. I can't say they were entirely wrong because if something triggered me emotionally, it meant there was an issue I needed to address, and life was showing it to me through others. As time passed, I worked on myself and improved by understanding my subconscious mind. However, the idea of mirroring was so ingrained in me that I developed a belief that "If you want to grow, there will be challenges, and people will reflect things to you."

Now, with this belief pattern, what do you think I attracted into my life? Yes, more tests! Because our subconscious thoughts create our reality. Would I have faced these tests if I believed growth and enlightenment would be easy and joyful? Probably not all of them. After understanding this, I distanced myself from people who tried to manipulate me by saying that awakening can only happen through strict tests and that everything is a reflection of me. Let me explain when the idea of mirroring becomes essential for awakening.

Suppose someone's actions cause you to feel a negative emotion (such as sadness, tension, anger, or jealousy). In that case, that's a situation where you should definitely examine what's going on in your subconscious. This shows that there are hidden emotions in your body and still waiting to be cleansed, and such adverse events trigger them, demanding you to empty yourself. In simple terms, instead of being angry at those people, you should thank them. They are unknowingly helping you to get rid of negative emotions, allowing you to discover your true self. The divine sends these experiences to help you change your feelings and beliefs and reconnect with your core being. It's not about causing you pain or suffering for no reason.

Now, let's say there is someone in front of you who is highly arrogant, and you are aware of it, but no emotion has arisen in you, and you have not been triggered. Is this person mirroring you again? NO!

At this stage, we need to be careful, or we might begin to criticize ourselves unfairly. It's not true that everyone and everything is always reflecting something on us. If there's no emotional reaction from your side, you don't get triggered and can simply observe the situation without getting involved. There's no need to overanalyze it or look for faults within yourself. The critical thing is, do you get emotionally triggered or not? If not, then move on. If yes, look at it; otherwise, you will repeatedly attract similar situations until it gets solved.

If you become more aware and find that some people in your life no longer fit your new way of thinking or have lower energy than you, the choice is yours. You can either accept it and continue to interact with them or recognize that they don't add value to your life and choose to keep your distance. At this stage, choosing to walk away is a way of standing up for yourself. It's not wrong to distance yourself from someone in this situation. You demonstrate that you are growing and improving by setting boundaries and recognizing your worth. Some worry that distancing themselves from others may lead to new challenges or create bad karma because they think they might cause harm. But this isn't true. It's natural for us to set our boundaries and choose to be around people who positively influence our lives. If you decide to stay around someone despite your concerns, whether out of guilt or fear of creating bad karma, you should be prepared to face the consequences of that choice because this is precisely what the divine wants from you: to know your worth. If you choose to distance yourself from someone and remove them from your life with love and understanding, then it's not a problem, and you won't create bad karma. The key is to do this with love and awareness. It's okay to recognize that your journey with someone has ended, and you don't need to cling to the relationship. Trust that new and better connections will come your way.

I've been through this many times. Whenever I ended long-term friendships because they weren't a good fit, new friends entered my life. And, of course, some of those blamed me for becoming arrogant or that I would have changed. Yes, indeed, I changed, not in their favor but mine.

Chapter IV

Conscious Living & Modern Challenges

Emotional Echoes: Deciphering Inherited Beliefs and Navigating the Landscape of Absorbed Emotions

At this point, I want to focus on the Emotions I mentioned above. People often don't realize that they can trap negative emotions created during a situation.

They might even take on someone else's negative feelings as their own. Over time, these trapped emotions build up inside them. Did you know that, on average, 70% of the emotions that exist in our bodies do not even belong to us?

That means the other way around is that only 30% of the emotions we carry in our body belong to us. The feelings we pick up from those around us can build up in our bodies and affect

us negatively, especially with health issues in the long term. Being aware of it, therefore, is very crucial.

I want to share a personal example. Before I was aware, I happily walked through crowds like supermarkets or spent time in cafes with friends, but when I left, I felt drained. I didn't realize then that I had unintentionally absorbed the emotions of others around me. I felt tired and also had difficulties waking up the next day. These were situations I couldn't understand why it was happening to me. Was I depressed all of a sudden? But what caused it? Two days ago, everything was fine. Am I maybe unbalanced? Questions, questions and exhaustion again.

I felt like I was learning and learning new teachings, but something I was doing wrong. Otherwise, I wouldn't be like this, right? So why does our body collect energies from others? I'll explain more about this later, but briefly, our body not only sends out energy and vibrations but also receives them. Imagine it like an Antenna. If you move through a crowd of people without being aware of this, you might end up feeling very tired and drained of energy by the end of the day.

How can you avoid this? Physical activities are vital to get rid of such energies. Movements such as sports, swimming, yoga, dance or running increase the body's energy and can help you eliminate negative emotions. Unfortunately, nowadays, people are getting lazy and unable to spare time for physical activities due to their work schedules. However, such actions will significantly contribute to keeping your body's energy high, your success and a healthier mind.

The tendency for people to affect each other with negative feelings has roots going back to the Stone Age. Back then, life was full of constant dangers, and people were not as safe as they are today.

They had to always be on the lookout for threats, whether from wars or other unexpected dangers that could come from any direction. During those times, cavemen needed to be aware of all possible threats to survive. Even a slight sound could frighten them, sending a warning signal to their brains that might protect them from a wild animal. This means that considering all possible outcomes and being cautious and pessimistic served to save their lives back then. Because of these experiences, humans carry a cellular memory filled with records of potential dangers from that era.

Science has discovered that traces of that time still exist in our cells and the primitive brain. This means people have been unconsciously programmed to think this way, leaning more toward negativity. The brain constantly looks for potential threats, not because it wants to be negative but because it's trying to keep us alive. It's an automatic response stemming from our ancient past. Today, we don't face threats like wild animals like lions or tigers. Instead, our brains see potential dangers in events like illness, accidents, financial struggles, or embarrassment during public speaking. The negative patterns inherited from our ancestors don't apply to our modern lives. However, our brains continue to follow this familiar pattern, creating new threats in our minds. This can lead many people to stress and anxiety. This tendency towards negative thinking often happens because people haven't developed their awareness and consciousness. You typically don't find such intense negativity in people who are more conscious of their thoughts. They have managed to change this negative thinking pattern in their brains. The good news is that this isn't set in stone for you. It's possible to change these thoughts and turn them into positive ones. The transformation starts with your desire and determination to make that change.

Looking at world history, it's clear that people everywhere have faced severe loss of life and property due to wars, diseases, famine, and other tragedies. As a result, many of us have an ingrained desire to ensure our safety, especially financially. This drive is rooted in our collective past, where our ancestors suffered significant losses. Without even realizing it, memories of these hardships are stored in our cellular memory, prompting us to seek financial security in our lives. Families mainly reflect this to their children and convey this lack of awareness without realizing it. Here's an example from my childhood, and I'll explain how it affected my life.

Growing up, I frequently witnessed my parents fighting over financial issues, driven mainly by my father's spending on alcohol and gambling. My mother even hid the money under the carpet to keep it out of his reach. Their disagreement about money issues was almost a daily routine and my brother and I, still just children, would often be reduced to tears, frightened and unable to comprehend the complex world of adult conflict. I prayed to God/Allah, begging that my parents wouldn't fight, if only for a day. My young and innocent mind began to harbor resentment toward God/Allah when my prayers seemed to go unanswered. I found it difficult to believe in Him, perceiving Him as unkind for allowing a child to endure such suffering. This early experience greatly influenced my struggle with faith in the Teenage Years.

This negative environment left a significant impact on me. My young mind interpreted money as the root cause of all the struggle and suffering in our home, leading me to develop a profound hatred for it. Unsurprisingly, this attitude translated into financial struggles later in life. Once I began earning my income, I found it challenging to retain money. It seemed to slip through my fingers, leaving me constantly in debt.

This lack of abundance mirrored my father's financial patterns, and it became clear that my subconscious was copying what it had learned during those formative years. I remained trapped in this cycle until I could identify and address the limiting belief about money that had been implanted in me as a child. Only then did I finally break free from the pattern of debt that had plagued me for so long.

I've since understood that my father and mother grew up in environments where money was always scarce. The narrative of financial loss was a common theme within my family, with many of my uncles consistently finding themselves in financial trouble. Even my grandfather would hide money from my grandmother. These patterns and behaviors within my family's history reveal a clear and recurring theme of financial insecurity and distrust, reflecting my struggles in my relationship with money.

This is just one example. Many of the beliefs and the mindset we have aren't ours. They're passed down to us through our DNA from our parents as our cells form in the womb. Additionally, the experiences stored in our subconscious from ages 0 to 6 form much of our lives.

Changing our consciousness is a complex task. We must work on our subconscious to transform the information stored in our cells. We can't move on to an entirely new life without clearing out everything we've unknowingly placed in our subconscious since birth, including the records we carry from our ancestors, mother and father. However, we can achieve lasting results beyond our dreams with patience, persistence and determination.

Digital Dominance: Realizing the Temptation and Traps of the Modern Age

As we move from the era of the caveman to the present day, we witnessed a transition from the analog world to the digital one. In the past, when even ordinary telephones didn't exist, we can now connect with the world through our devices. Cell phones have evolved into smartphones and have begun to dominate our lives. Many individuals, often without conscious awareness, have become overly dependent on their digital devices. This addiction extends to various aspects of daily life, such as during meals, restroom breaks, before bedtime and after waking up in the morning. A 2016 study by Common Sense Media found that 50% of teenagers feel addicted to their mobile devices, which can contribute to antisocial behavior because most of them spend an average of nine hours a day on their smartphones, according to the same study's results.

Studies have shown that even adult addiction to mobile devices is a growing concern in modern society. Research conducted by the American Psychological Association unveils that adults who overuse mobile devices experience higher stress levels, sleep disturbances and a decrease in face-to-face social interactions. The constant connection to

work, social media and online entertainment can lead to an imbalance in personal and professional life. This reliance on technology underscores the need for mindful usage and awareness of potential negative impacts on mental and physical well-being.

Unfortunately, this has led to an increase in the number of people who are less engaged in face-to-face conversations and more absorbed in their screens. Especially the new generation has been exposed to this a lot because they were born into the digital world. People born before the year 2000 have had some exposure to the analog world, which may have helped them partially resist this dependency on digital devices. Nonetheless, a substantial portion of society has developed a severe addiction to their smartphones. It became a reflex for many to reach for their phone almost every minute, whether to check social media or read messages. This behavior has become a pattern as the brain got permanently used to it. When addiction is mentioned, most people immediately think of substances like alcohol, drugs or food. However, in the modern era, especially for those born after the year 2000, many unnoticed addictions are taking root, like smartphone usage. Reflecting on the previous passage, one might ask: How many times a day do you take your phone to check your social media and messages? How often do you monitor the number of likes on a picture you've shared? These habits indicate a new form of addiction that has become ingrained in our daily lives. And there's a hidden danger in this digital immersion that many of us may not recognize: the digital world is dominating our lives. For instance, seeing someone enjoying a vacation on social media while you're stuck in the office can demotivate and drain your energy for the rest of the day. The moment you begin comparing your life to those who seem to be living better through their social media posts, you set yourself up for feelings of unhappiness and dissatisfaction. Before the era of the digital world, people simply shared their photo albums with friends and family. In today's digital age, we have instant access to what people do worldwide through social media. We can now see what individuals in distant countries eat, wear and how they live, leading us to compare and sometimes even imitate their lives. This constant comparison can overshadow our appreciation for our own lives. Individuals constantly measure themselves against one another: Who had the most beautiful vacation? Who drives the fancier car? Who seems most fulfilled in their romantic relationship? Who appears to lead the most enviable life? Only if we can get out of this race can we start to meet our inner divinity.

These constant comparisons divert us from our true selves and prevent us from living in the present moment. While on vacation, instead of relishing the beautiful surroundings, many individuals are preoccupied with their phones, repeatedly checking social media and other distractions, thus failing to enjoy their time off fully. People often spend their holidays sharing pictures online and obsessing over how many likes they receive. Later, they complain about how quickly time has flown by, feeling like they've missed out on truly experiencing their vacation. Here's another example: When you gather with friends at a table, observe how many phones are out and how often the conversation is interrupted by people glancing at their devices. Sadly, these are the new norms of today's society. However, if we are mindful and aware of our actions, we don't have to fall into these patterns, and we can break free from these habits.

Let's also mention the negative impact of this behavior on our brains. Since our brain operates mainly subconsciously when we first wake up, exposure to negative news during the first hour can set a negative tone for the rest of the day. So, what's the first thing you do when you wake up in the morning? If it's reaching for your phone, your

brain is immediately bombarded with dozens of information. This can lead to starting your day in a chaotic and uncentered state without even realizing it.

Looking at screens before bedtime can negatively impact your sleep quality. The constant downward gaze can lead to neck pain, and your eyes may become fatigued from extended screen time. This can delay the body's natural recovery process at night, leading to additional discomfort and potentially affecting your overall well-being. The time we spend constantly holding our phones is another concern. Instead of engaging in beneficial activities like reading a book, meditating, praying, educating ourselves, exercising, or having meaningful conversations with loved ones, we often find ourselves caught up in watching the lives of others. As we keep watching one thing after another, the brain goes into autopilot, and before we know it, hours have passed.

Rather than getting lost in the virtual world, you could go to the gym to nurture your body, resulting in a fitter and more vital you. Meditation allows you to tune in to your inner voice and connect to the Divine. By exploring new hobbies, you can cultivate personal growth in various fields. By engaging in these constructive activities, you not only motivate yourself but also become a source of inspiration to others.

In addition to these concerns, you're also exposed to the electromagnetic fields caused by these devices, absorbing these energies into your body. Essentially, various actions and behaviors that can diminish your vibrational frequency are channeled to you through this single device. In engaging with it in this way, you may be unintentionally causing harm to yourself without even realizing the impact.

Shift your consciousness in this realm so that you don't become enslaved by the digital world, allowing a mere device to determine your happiness, peace and overall life experience. Do not let the allure of advertisements, images of people living seemingly happier lives, or the glitz of celebrities overly influence you. Recognize that all these factors can significantly negatively impact your subconscious mind and lead to less gratitude, as I said before.

And if you find yourself trapped in endless comparisons with others through social media, asking questions like "Why can they go on vacation and I can't?", "Why does he have a girlfriend and I don't?" or "Why does she seem to live more comfortably than me?" try to raise awareness and think of all the gifts in life you already have. And that includes being healthy. Don't let this constant measuring against others diminish your gratitude towards your life, leading to frustration.

Conscious Consumption: Understanding Our Subconscious Desires and Taking Responsibility

In a world driven by consumption, we are encouraged to buy more than we truly need. This has led to excessive consumption of the world's resources, from plastics polluting the oceans to the deforestation and endangerment of various species. Often, our shopping decisions aren't based on genuine needs but are influenced by advertisements, marketing strategies and social pressures, especially in the era of social media and the digital world.

My goal here isn't to make anyone feel guilty but to foster greater awareness. I used to be unaware of these issues, often buying things I didn't need. When I felt sad or depressed, I would shop to distract myself, mistakenly believing that I could purchase happiness. Now, I understand that such behavior was misguided. Being uninformed isn't a fault; the real problem lies in knowing something but failing to act on that knowledge.

This happens because our subconscious mind controls us. Even when we're aware of our actions, our primitive instincts can influence our behavior, such as when we shop.

People often crave the latest phone model or the trendiest clothing, and some even go so far as to borrow money to acquire the most up-to-date technology. But why is this? At the root of this desire, there's often a hidden motivation that the subconscious mind is trying to fulfill. Many individuals aspire to emulate those they follow on social media, seeking to look and feel like them.

We often dismiss our responsibility with excuses like, "Can I really make a difference in this World? Will my actions change anything?" Imagine if, for example, three billion people in the world were to think this way simultaneously.

It's a perspective that can have a significant impact. Our world is in its current state partly because so many people say, "What can I accomplish on my own?" But if we each take responsibility for our actions and choices, we can create a collective shift in global awareness.

Industries create products to meet our demands, and if we don't make conscious purchasing decisions, they will continue to use the world's resources without restraint. We, as consumers, have the power to influence this, but often, we give up that power and allow ourselves to be dictated by industry trends. So, what's the path forward? How can we define and practice conscious consumption? How does this concept connect with our core values and the greater scope of our existence?

Have you ever found yourself in this situation? You purchase something and later question why, perhaps even regretting it once you get home or receive the package. Think about the unused items in your house, bought impulsively. People might have ten pairs of shoes but consistently reach for their two favorite pairs because they're the most comfortable. The others may only be worn once a month or less frequently. Yet, they feel free to buy the eleventh pair when they see a discount or a great deal. It's not about placing blame or assuming everyone does this; it's about raising awareness of our shopping habits and their reasons.

Do you genuinely need the items you purchase? If the answer is "No", why do we often feel compelled to acquire more than we need? Social perceptions and societal influences play a significant role in shaping these desires. TV shows, advertisements, and social media posts subconsciously influence us. Products are presented as essential to our lives

and these messages embed themselves in our subconscious minds. Later, we may purchase the exact same products, believing they'll make us as happy as the woman in the commercial or as successful as the man in the TV show.

Behind many of our shopping decisions, there's often an underlying emotion or experience we're seeking to capture and live. We constantly attempt to satisfy our inner emptiness with temporary joy, such as unnecessary shopping. Once we find genuine happiness and grow awareness, we'll quickly recognize that lasting pleasure and satisfaction cannot be achieved through shopping, and we'll no longer feel the need for it. Therefore, conscious consumption plays a vital role in knowing ourselves, understanding our needs and noticing our emotions. When we discover true happiness, we meet our essence and get closer to our infinity. Rather than impulsively purchasing items, we make more conscious decisions to bring new things into our lives.

Think about what feelings are connected to the things you buy, like clothes, gadgets or eating out. Often, people shop more when they're unhappy, especially women, trying to eliminate negative emotions. But this is just an illusion. It would be best if you confronted what's making you unhappy; otherwise, you'll be trapped in this falsehood and never discover your true potential within you and that is the Divinity hidden inside.

When discussing consumption, it's not only about the things we buy. It also includes our daily choices, such as whom we follow on social media and how we spend our time with others. Time is our most precious resource, so how we choose to spend it is incredibly important. As we age, we often start to think more about the time we have left and how we want to spend it. But as we progress on the path to enlightenment, we may come to realize, as Einstein once said, that time is relative. While our journey on this planet will one day come to an end, our existence in the infinite universe will continue in a different form. What truly matters is how we choose to exit this stage of life when the time comes. Many people complain about the past, filled with regret about things they did or didn't do, while others worry excessively about the future. Both of these mindsets rob you of your precious time in the present. That's why it's often said that living in the moment is the only way to experience life to the fullest. To live fully in the present, you must free yourself from the burdens of the past and worries about the future. This requires letting go of hidden emotions and finding peace within yourself. How can you achieve this peace?

By forgiving yourself! It's often easier to forgive others than to forgive yourself for past mistakes. Learning to forgive myself was the most challenging part of my journey toward enlightenment. I found it much easier to forgive others than myself. The thought that I had allowed others to hurt, scam, or disrespect me was unbearable. How could I let that happen? This is the point where my mind became stuck in the past, replaying scenarios over and over again, thinking about what I would have said if I were the person I am now. The anger inside me was so intense that it felt like it was eating me from the inside.

Because of this anger energy, that I carried with me, guess what happened? I was frequently attracted to situations in my life where I can feel angry. For example, fighting with a driver who took my right-of-way in traffic would enrage me beyond belief. There were times when I would shout at those people. Now I realize that I was not yelling at them but at myself. I was so angry with myself that I created these kinds of situations in my life.

Take a look at your own life. Are there moments when you are mad and angry at yourself and take it out on someone else? Perhaps it's your family, friends, employees or even strangers. Recognizing this anger and understanding where it's directed can be crucial to self-awareness and growth. You have to know that as long as you don't release your negative emotions, these emotions will attract situations for you so they can show up. And it will constantly ruin your life if you don't release them. That's why it is always said that you can never attract happiness and joy out of anger and sadness. Both are different frequencies that don't match. It is like waiting for a train at the bus station.

Mindful Consumption: Navigating Nutrition and Finding Balance in a World of Excess

Along with other forms of consumption, food is another critical aspect. I'd like to take a moment to discuss nutrition and our bodies, as this field is filled with conflicting information. It becomes challenging to know what to believe. For example, one nutrition expert might advocate that eating eggs is healthy, while another insists that eggs are unhealthy. Previously, it was widely believed that drinking milk would strengthen bones. However, recent studies, including some cited by the National Library of Medicine, have raised questions about this assumption, with some findings even suggesting that milk consumption could contribute to osteoporosis. The relationship between milk consumption and osteoporosis is complex and has been the subject of various studies with differing conclusions. Some research suggests that milk and other dairy products might contribute to bone health due to their calcium and vitamin D content. Other studies have raised questions about whether high milk consumption might be linked to osteoporosis or other health problems. So now, which one shall we believe? There's also a growing trend towards a vegan lifestyle, where all animal products are avoided. It is everyone's own choice. I want to emphasize the need to be mindful of the food we consume, as our body is the temple in which we live. Without our bodies, we cannot exist on this planet. Our body acts as an antenna for energies, as explained before, and it also serves as an antenna to connect to our Soul. Therefore, our health is directly tied to our awareness of our body. How can we look after our bodies when an overwhelming amount of information about nutrition and wellness is available? The critical point to recognize is that everybody is unique and has different needs. However, it is widely understood that our bodies do not require industrially processed sugar, carbonated beverages, chocolate and similar items. To maintain health, the body fundamentally needs four things: oxygen, water, minerals and vitamins. Our eating habits, often learned from our families, can influence how we fulfill these needs. We might even continue some of these habits subconsciously.

It's time to challenge all the conflicting information out there. I'm not here to dictate what you should or shouldn't eat; that's something you need to discover for yourself based on what's good or bad for your body. I can only share my personal experience. For example, since significantly reducing my consumption of milk, sugar and meat, I've noticed that my skin looks healthier and I wake up earlier feeling more energetic in the morning. My energy level is now relatively high. Sometimes, my followers comment, "My energy is down; is there negative energy affecting me?" I often respond, "Have you been drinking enough water? Have you taken the necessary supplements? Have you checked your blood levels at least once a year?" Attributing every instance of low energy to spiritual negative energy is inaccurate.

Increase your awareness of your physical health and mindful eating habits. Conduct your own research and implement what feels suitable for your body. Every person's body is unique and has different needs. Make gradual changes in this area rather than radical ones, as your body has gotten used to a particular consumption pattern. If you suddenly change this pattern, your body might be shocked, leaving you tired and unmotivated. For instance, if you're used to consuming much sugar, reducing it gradually rather than all at once is wise. Also, if you desire something that will benefit your

body and well-being you can consume it. However, it's important to remember that over-eating can lead to losing balance.

It's similar to the situation where you insist on having a second plate after enjoying a plate of food, even though it might be more than you need. In this situation, your subconscious mind may drive you to eat more. You might give in to this urge and then feel guilty after eating that second plate. Perhaps you regret it and become angry with yourself. Because there's often a lack of awareness about these impulses, we might unconsciously choose to eat what our subconscious craves rather than our body needs, for example, opting for pasta when a healthy salad might be the better choice. If we feel a lot of emotional hunger and deal with emotions like anger, sadness, or excessive joy, we may resort to a more unbalanced or unhealthy diet. This could lead to weight gain.

An example might be the guilt we feel after eating bags of chips or chocolate, followed by the extra weight accumulating in our bodies. At this point, it's helpful to ask ourselves what we are really trying to satisfy. What are we attempting to digest emotionally, or what do we genuinely consume when eating?

Sometimes, individuals have such a buildup of emotions that they attempt to process them through eating. However, this cycle won't shift unless one addresses their subconscious. Firstly, we must release the negative emotions (like anger, resentment, sadness, grief, fears, and so on) stored within us. This is the essential thing that you will read over and over again in this book.

Desiring more than we truly need can turn into a form of emotional greed. I'm not suggesting that you should limit your enjoyment or never ask for anything extra. I'm trying to convey that if your basic needs are satisfied and you feel a sense of harmony and balance, you don't necessarily have to consume more than you need.

Why am I telling you all of this? To discover our essence and infinity within us depends on being able to see the whole picture and raise your awareness. And that is the way to the divine within us. I'm trying to convey that if your basic needs are satisfied and you feel a sense of harmony and balance, you don't necessarily need to consume more than you need..

*"Body is purified by water.
Ego by tears. Intellect is
purified by knowledge.
And Soul is purified with Love."*
- Imam Ali

Chapter V

Mind, Brain & Inner Universe

The Magic Within: Unraveling the Secrets of Our DNA and Tracing Our Ancestral Footprints

How aware are we of our bodies' vital role in our existence? Do we truly understand the importance of taking care of our bodies? Are we conscious of how poor nutrition, stress, lack of physical activity, the constant use of our phones and radiation exposure can seriously impact our well-being? When our bodies are unwell, how can

we uncover our true essence and potential? How can we hope to transform and reach for our dreams when we're struggling with low energy, confined to our beds or couches, and consumed by TV shows instead of pursuing our passions?

Achieving enlightenment is unattainable if you overlook this topic, as spirituality cannot thrive without a body that is functioning well. Only then can you level up your energy and frequency, and only then can you improve your Life Quality.

So, at this point, I want to go deeper into our Body, which is a miracle in itself. It's important to recognize and be aware of the magnetic field generated by our hearts. Similarly, we must understand how our brain functions and learn its connection to spirituality and infinity. To uncover our true nature, we need to comprehend how our body operates. This understanding will help us recognize why changing ourselves requires significant effort and work, allowing us to develop ourselves consciously. Having fundamental knowledge about the human body will benefit this process.

A beautiful proverb says, "To know one's future, one must first understand the past." With that wisdom in mind, let's travel back in time to explore what the DNA within our bodies reveals about our ancestry. Research conducted at institutions like Stanford University has established that our genes hold all the genetic records of our existence, also covering the legacy of our ancestors. People have migrated and relocated throughout history, leading to a rich blend of genetic heritage. For example, you might have been born in Turkiye, but if you trace back seven generations or more, where do your ancestors originate from? What were they doing in the 13th century? Or the 5th century? While we often limit our understanding of ancestry to our grandparents, the reality is that the information stored in our cells goes back much further, painting a fascinating picture of our familial history.

Did you know that inside every single cell of our body, there is a two-meter-long DNA helix that holds the codes of our ancestors, essentially our genetic heritage? You can think of the cell as a

vast library, and the DNA within it is related to the detailed information found on the pages of the books in that library.

According to research, the storage capacity of DNA is incredibly huge. A study by Harvard University highlighted that just one gram of DNA could potentially contain a massive amount of information. To illustrate this, consider a typical HD movie that takes up 6 gigabytes on a DVD. The information in one gram of DNA could theoretically be equivalent to millions of these DVDs. It's a fascinating way to understand how complex and information-rich our genetic code is. Each human body consists of approximately 100 trillion cells, and almost every cell has about two meters of DNA inside (excluding about 25 percent of blood cells). If you were to lay out all of this DNA end to end, it would stretch for an astonishing 150 billion kilometers. This distance is so huge that it would be like traveling between the Earth and the sun 1000 times, according to the National Human Genome Research Institute. It's a staggering illustration of the complexity and marvel of the human body. Are you now aware of how much information is stored in your body?

I want to give you another example. If you were to try to count the cells in the human body, adding one cell every second, it would take an incredibly long time to reach the total number. One source even estimates it would take 3 million years to do so (Spectrum Akademischer Verlag, Heidelberg). This gives us another perspective on the staggering complexity of the human body.

Everything, including our cells, is composed of atoms. Consider the vast number of atoms and their space within our body; it's a staggering concept to grasp. Have you now noticed what kind of miracle your body contains? Our seemingly small bodies include a vast universe within that we often overlook. To keep us alive, our cells perform an incredible array of tasks. They rejuvenate our skin, circulate oxygen through our blood and create reproductive cells like eggs and sperm to perpetuate life. These are just a few examples; our cells also repair damaged tissues, aid in digestion, fight off infections and regulate our body temperature, among many other essential functions.

Did you know that in the human body, an estimated tens of millions of cells die every second? This natural process is known as apoptosis or programmed cell death. While this number might seem significant, it's a small fraction of the trillions of cells in our body. Importantly, our body also generates new cells roughly the same rate as old ones die off. Although it's often said that we have a "new" body every seven years, this is a simplification. Different cells have different lifespans, with some being replaced rapidly and others lasting much longer. Thus, while certain body parts may renew frequently, others do not, making the renewal process complex and ongoing.

Next, I'd like to explore other essential functions within our body. Understanding these will shed light on why subconscious connections and changes often take considerable time to materialize. These insights can open up the way for transforming your life more easily and making the process more accessible. Unfortunately, many people emphasize spirituality while overlooking these vital details. This oversight can lead to frustration and self-blame, with thoughts like, "Why isn't my life changing?" Awareness of our body's complex workings can help avoid such misunderstandings and empower us to shift positively in our lives.

The Marvel of the Nervous System: The Power of Our Habits

The nervous system is an amazing network of nerves and cells with high complexity that transmit signals between different parts of the body. It's divided into two main parts: the central nervous system (CNS) and the peripheral nervous system (PNS). The CNS is part of the brain and spinal cord, while the PNS covers all the nerves that are distributed from the CNS to the rest of the body.

This remarkable nervous system that our body houses continuously sends signals at astonishing speeds, ranging from 150 to 434 kilometers per hour, as per research by the University of California. This intricate system, with the brain and spinal cord at its control center, manages massive functions.

You can compare the spinal cord to a major highway, with commands from the brain spreading signals across the entire body. According to Munich Clinic, this network, whose total length might reach 5.8 million kilometers, oversees the distribution of information and commands, vital functions like breathing, heartbeat, and blood flow, motor movements such as lifting a hand or eating with a fork, emotional responses and muscle movements.

Through precisely coordinating these tasks, the nervous system ensures that our bodies respond and function seamlessly, from the most vital processes that sustain life to the subtle gestures that express our humanity. This grand orchestration of biological signals is a testament to human physiology's marvel.

Like the continuous flow of digital communication through the internet, there is an unending interaction within our body facilitated by signals sent through neurons. For instance, if a specific scent triggers memories that make you feel happy, sad, or nostalgic, it's all because of the signals originating from the brain. These connections enable us to respond and react to our environment in ways that are both complex and deeply personal.

So, what is our nervous system made of? Like everything else in our body, the nervous system is composed of cells. But a unique feature sets these cells apart: they carry an electrical charge. These electrically charged cells are known as neurons, derived from ancient Greek word for "nerve". According to the Max-Planck Institute, an estimated 100 billion neurons exist in the human brain alone. This electrical charge is essential, as, without it, the signals within our body would not be able to reach their destinations. Think of it like a power outage-

no devices can function when the electricity goes off. Similarly, without this neural electricity, our body's internal communication would come to a blockage.

Neurons in our brains are continually talking to one another. Every thought we have creates a reflection in these neurons, and the more we focus on a specific thought, the stronger the connection between the neurons becomes. You can think of it like a rope - the more strands you add to it, the stronger it gets. For instance, if we constantly worry about something, we train our bodies to be anxious. We then continually attract situations to worry about, a principle that aligns with the law of attraction or resonance. Since our cells respond to what we think and feel, we send out vibrations that reflect our anxiety, drawing more of it into our lives. Let's consider the example of phone addiction. Every time we reach for our phone, a neurological signal travels from our brain to our hands. The

more we repeat this action, the stronger that connection becomes, eventually becoming a habit. This is why our hand starts to reach for the phone almost automatically.

In essence, the more you repeat an action, the more it becomes ingrained in your cells through the neurons in your brain, eventually becoming a habit. This principle applies to all aspects of life, not just phone usage. For example, patterns such as your eating habits, reading routines, taking the same route to work, frequenting the same places and engaging in physical exercise. Repeated actions create pathways in the brain, reinforcing these habits over time. That's why the words you say to yourself are so important. When you say, "I hope nothing bad happens today to me", you give a negative command to your brain without realizing it, and then you really start to attract what you have in your mind. In fact, we are doing the most extensive sabotage to ourselves. A word like "I'd rather die than live like this..." and similar sentences can seriously affect our lives. These are contracts we make with ourselves without even knowing it. If you once firmly declare that you will never love again, you shouldn't be surprised if you struggle to find the love of your life later on, even after you've forgotten that vow. While saying something negative just once doesn't necessarily shape our lives, repeating it frequently can have a real impact. The example highlights the importance of being mindful of what we repeatedly say, as it might unintentionally influence our future.

So how to use Affirmation correctly? Many people attempt affirmations without achieving lasting effects. Why does this happen? If deep-rooted limiting beliefs persist, affirmations like "I attract money wherever I go" may not work. I've experienced this frustration myself, feeling as if my efforts were fruitless. The key is to clear the subconscious mind and emotions first, then apply affirmations. Without this essential step, it's like pouring clean water into a cup filled with dirty water.

Below are some affirmations you might find helpful. Repeat them at least 21 times daily, or even 108 times as suggested in ancient teachings, to imprint them on your subconscious. Remember that repetition is the Master of Skills.

Affirmations:

- *I'm fortunate today.*
- *Life sends me a lot of gifts.*
- *I attract money wherever I go.*
- *I live a life beyond miracles and magic.*

- *All of Life comes to me with ease, joy and glory.*
- *Every day and in every way, I am getting better and better.*

The subconscious mind operates in the present and doesn't recognize the concept of time. Therefore, when communicating with the subconscious, for example, with affirmations, it's crucial to use the present tense rather than future terms like "I will." Phrases that are ambiguous in timing may not have the desired effect because everything in the subconscious happens in the "now". Many teachings emphasize the importance

of being present at the moment, as creation and change can only happen from this immediate standpoint.

The Transformative Power of Neuroplasticity: Understanding the Brain's Ability to Adapt and Learn

As I mentioned repeatedly about patterns and habits, I want first to clarify the difference between the two words before we move on. While a habit refers to a specific repeated behavior or practice by an individual, a pattern is a more general term that can refer to repeated designs or behaviors found in various contexts, not limited to personal routines or actions. Habits are often considered a subset of patterns as they involve repeated behaviors, but patterns encompass a more comprehensive array of repeated or regular occurrences. When you repeat something over and over again, especially a behavior or action, you are typically building a habit, which is made up through neurons in our brain. At this point, I would like to talk to you about Neuroplasticity.

Neuroplasticity can be broken down into two parts. "Neuro" relates to the neurons, while "plasticity" derives from the ancient Greek word "plassein", which means variability and the ability to be transformed. The term "Neuroplasticity" refers to the adaptability and changeable nature of the brain's structure by forming new neural connections. This adaptability enables the brain to compensate for injury, disease, or environmental changes. It's central to learning new skills, remembering experiences and adapting to new situations. In essence, Neuroplasticity illustrates the brain's remarkable capacity to change and evolve throughout an individual's lifetime.

Scientific research has demonstrated that it is possible for us to positively alter and restructure our brains and even rebuild neuronal networks. One example of this is a study conducted on London taxi drivers. These individuals were found to have increased neurological activity and brain plasticity (despite being adults) because of their need to learn about London's complex traffic system. This discovery shows that the human brain can adapt and change in response to specific requirements, supporting the idea of Neuroplasticity.

Enhancing neuroplasticity means the brain can adapt more quickly to new information and learn more easily. Whether it's acquiring multiple languages as an adult, undergoing further training or exploring novel skills, our brain is inherently prepared to embrace new learning experiences.

The more we engage in these activities, the more we enhance our brain's adaptability and learning capacity, promoting further growth in Neuroplasticity.

As you embrace the opportunity to learn new things, your brain becomes more engaged and agile. While there is a common misconception that "you can only learn when you're young," this is not entirely accurate. The reality is that there's no age limit to learning. The challenge in acquiring new skills or knowledge as we get older is not due to our brain's inability or reduced capacity to learn but rather a difficulty in focusing and concentrating. So you have to be patient with yourself. Just as going to the gym to lose weight and gain muscle requires time, discipline and repetition, the same principles apply to training our brains.

The brain's cells can be activated through our will, but if we cultivate a habit of laziness, our brain may also become lazy and struggle to take action. By breaking this cycle, we can utilize our brains more effectively and efficiently.

The critical point here is to stimulate our brain's capacity, as we have both active and passive neuron connections. Passive connections come from areas of our brain that go unused. For

example, if an adult merely goes to work every day without learning anything new, the unused parts of the brain become inactive. This leads to a failure to utilize a significant portion of the brain's capacity, even though much more potential exists within it.

To give another example, musicians appear to have more neurological activity in specific brain regions compared to non-musicians.

Indeed, our own limiting beliefs can create barriers to learning. If we adopt a negative mindset, thinking, "How can I possibly learn something new at my age?" we can unintentionally hold ourselves back. But, scientific research, including a study from the Max-Planck Institute, has shown that the brain does not age as long as it continues to learn. So, no matter our age, by embracing new learning experiences, we can keep our brain structure vibrant and active, enhancing our Neuroplasticity and our overall mental vitality.

Just as we engage in physical activities like workouts to keep our bodies healthy and fit, we must also do mental exercises to keep the neurons in our brains active. Not all neurons are in constant use; some remain passive or dormant. The less we engage and train these neurons, the more they become inactive. Active neurons consume more energy, requiring more oxygen and glucose and thus attracting more blood flow to their location. In contrast, passive neurons that remain inactive are starved of energy, and since the brain sees them as unnecessary, they can eventually die off. Therefore, maintaining an active brain is vital to keeping all neurons functioning and healthy.

Why is understanding neurons essential when it comes to habits? Because the key to our habits lies in these neurons. To grasp how we can change our habits, we must first understand what neurons are and how they function. You need to eliminate the negative patterns that hold you back to uncover your true potential. Whether it's a desire to meditate that's consistently postponed, longing to start exercising, lose weight, or adopt healthier habits, procrastination often forms the primary barrier to our goals. Understanding the neural basis of procrastination can be an essential step toward overcoming these barriers and achieving our desired habits.

At this point, the way neurons communicate with each other becomes crucial. Imagine you consciously want to watch a different movie and change the television channel, but your brain automatically keeps you on the current channel, continuing to watch the same movie. Think of your brain as having the remote control; it's the control center with the power to dictate your actions. Until you recognize this control, it won't be easy to break free from your habits. Understanding the neuronal basis of this automatic response is critical to changing enrooted routines and preferences.

If you want to grow and improve yourself, especially spiritually, you need to reconfigure these connections between neurons to align with your desired outcomes. To accomplish this, it's essential to recognize the importance of your thoughts. Neurons communicate with each other every time you think; the more you concentrate on a particular thought, the stronger those neural connections become. This reinforcement of connections can translate your thoughts into reality, shaping your actions and behaviors by what you consistently focus on.

In essence, a habit is a reflection of our recurring thoughts. If you consistently concentrate on negative thoughts and anticipate what could go wrong, you're cultivating a habit that can hold you back. This habitual negativity trains your brain to think pessimistically. To break free from this pattern, you must shift your mindset and perspective on life, allowing you to transform these ingrained habits within your brain. When we think of habits, we often consider physical routines like waking up at eight for work, eating the same meals, or visiting familiar places. However, habits also encompass recurring patterns like consistently attracting similar people into our lives, saying "Yes" when we mean "No", prioritizing others' needs, or frequently feeling stressed. In essence, any behavior we perform automatically and subconsciously becomes a habit by repetition. Realizing this fact is essential because it allows you to see how many negative habits you may have. With this awareness, you can work to transform negative patterns into positive ones. This transformation can lead to attracting people who enrich your life, cultivating love and respect, and developing new habits in areas such as financial abundance, relationships, healthy eating and more.

Here are some strategies to help you change your habits:

1.) Identify the Habit: First, recognize the specific habit you want to overcome.

2.) Understand Triggers and Emotions: Take note of the situations and emotions that trigger your habit. Is it stress that leads you to smoke, or boredom that causes you to reach for junk food?

3.) Analyze the Habit: Ask yourself why you engage in these behaviors. What feelings are you trying to escape from? By understanding the underlying emotions, you realize that the habit (like smoking or watching TV) is just a way to cope with those feelings.

4.) Learn to Stop Yourself: Once you know these triggers, stop yourself just before falling back into that habit. It's hard to resist, as your brain is wired to repeat familiar actions. Realizing this can help you to break the cycle.

5.) Utilize Neuroplasticity: Now that you understand the brain's ability to change, you can work to reinforce positive neural connections.

These steps provide a clear pathway to understanding and altering habits, focusing on self-awareness and the brain's ability to adapt.

Enhancing Neuroplasticity: Practical Tips and Exercise

1.) Juggling: Believe it or not, juggling is a potent exercise to boost neuroplasticity. It helps connect the right and left brain lobes and positively affects the brain's structure. Just grab three balls and practice for a few minutes daily. If I can learn and enjoy it, so can you, especially now that you know your brain is capable of it.

2.) Brush Your Teeth with the Opposite Hand: If you usually brush with your right hand, try using your left or vice versa. This simple switch helps your brain adapt to something new, stimulating neuroplasticity.

3.) Cross-Ear Hand Exercise: Place your right hand on your left ear and your left hand on your right ear. Then, bend your knees and move up and down for one minute. This unique exercise can also enhance your brain's adaptability.

4.) Engage in Mindfulness or Meditation Practices: Mindfulness exercises and meditation focus on controlling thoughts and awareness, helping to create new connections within the brain. Regular practice can enhance concentration, emotional regulation and cognitive flexibility, contributing to increased neuroplasticity.

5.) Learning a New Musical Instrument: Picking up a musical instrument stimulates different brain areas, even if you've never played one before. Learning to read music and coordinating your hands to create melodies challenges the brain in new and complex ways, promoting neuroplasticity.

Integrating these exercises into your daily or weekly routine can provide a varied and engaging way to foster positive changes in your brain's structure and function.

"The mind is like a parachute. It only works if it's open."
- James Dewar

Exploring the Science and Spirituality of the "Third Eye": Gateway to Higher Consciousness or Mystical Metaphor?

Despite ongoing research, the human brain remains largely a mystery. Some experts estimate we have only uncovered about 10% - 30% of its functionality today. Our current technology is still insufficient to grasp the complexity of the brain's functions fully, leading scientists to update and revise their findings continually. Each new study gains fresh insights, and previously accepted information may become outdated. Similar to the enigmas of the universe, the entire understanding of the human brain continues to elude scientific explanation.

And one of the continuing enigmas in our understanding of the brain is the small Pineal Gland. Before going deeper into the many spiritual connections attributed to the pineal gland, it's essential to lay a solid foundation by examining what science has revealed about this intriguing part of the brain. By understanding its scientifically recognized functions and characteristics, we can better appreciate the mystique and spiritual interpretations that surround it. Let's first take a closer look at the scientific aspect of the pineal gland.

Located centrally within the brain, this gland is the size of a rice grain and has a shape that resembles a pine cone.

One of the functions of the pineal gland is to manage the balance between sleep and wakefulness. It does this by controlling the levels of two hormones: melatonin, which helps us fall asleep, and serotonin, often called the "happiness hormone". On average, the pineal gland measures between 5 and 8 mm. It is believed to be most active during the night, particularly between 2 and 3 am, although this timing can vary among individuals. Be aware that the specific hours of activity and the detailed functioning of the pineal gland are complex and not completely understood.

In some alternative health circles, there's a belief that poor nutrition (such as consuming too much sugar or pre-packaged ready-to-eat foods) and fluoride exposure can significantly impact the pineal gland by causing calcification. This calcification is a process where calcium phosphate deposits build up in different parts of the gland. This well-documented phenomenon can be observed in many individuals as they age. However, the scientific evidence is insufficient to make definitive statements about the relationship between diet, fluoride and pineal gland function.

So now, let's build the bridge between science and spirituality here. The pineal gland has a long and fascinating history that extends beyond scientific understanding into spirituality and mysticism. In many ancient civilizations, this gland was referred to as the "organ of God", it has been associated with intuition, foresight and a connection to spiritual dimensions. Many believe it represents the "third eye" or "sixth sense".

What makes this gland particularly astounding is its physical resemblance to an eye. Positioned deep within the brain, the pineal gland's shape and structure have been compared to the human eye's. Some examinations have even found similarities between the internal structure of the pineal gland and the eye's retina, including similar fluids. This may be why it is associated with an invisible "third eye" that we possess without full awareness. Discovering the nature of this third eye and understanding how intuition operates can be a profound journey. Unfortunately, many individuals become stuck in their thoughts, unable to perceive the subtle guidance of their souls. And I believe that intuition is our Soul's whisper that guides us through life's complexities and connects us with the inner divinity.

With all this information, we must understand that this tiny gland in our brain can be essential to discovering our Soul and Infinity. Although science has not been able to unravel all the functions of the pineal gland, it is believed that this gland is the home of our soul, the gateway to the universe and higher dimensions.

Some spiritual teachings claim that individuals who fully utilize the capacity of the pineal gland can access profound intuition and even experience astral travel. Essentially, the pineal gland is perceived as a gateway to higher consciousness and spiritual awakening. Practices like meditation and specific yogic traditions are designed to "activate" or "awaken" the third eye, aiming to deepen spiritual understanding and enhance inner insight.

Though these spiritual associations are widespread and deeply rooted in many cultures, it's essential to note that scientific research has not definitively proven many of these beliefs. And this is where Science and Spirituality split their ways. Because you can not get for every mystique teaching and event a scientific answer. At one point it is belief. Do you think for example, that one day Science can measure or see our pure Soul or even the Divine? I doubt that, but it's worth a try by Science. Some might think one day it's possible, but I believe it is impossible. I leave it up to you what you think.

Some believe the pineal gland is oriented towards the heavens or the universe, symbolizing a connection to higher spiritual realms. This belief is reflected in various ancient civilizations, where symbols resembling a pine cone, thought to represent the pineal gland, are found. For example, in ancient Egypt, the "Eye of Horus", a symbol of protection and wisdom, has been linked to the pineal gland by some researchers. In ancient Rome, the pine cone symbol was used in art and architecture, and a giant bronze pine cone called "Pigna" still stands in the Vatican.

The Aztecs and other Mesoamerican cultures also featured pine cone symbols in their art, and some interpretations connect these with spiritual insight or enlightenment.

So, we have to understand that the pineal gland has been associated with spirituality, particularly within various esoteric, mystical, and New Age teachings rather than from science. Nevertheless, the recurring appearance of this symbol across different cultures and the connections drawn to the pineal gland contribute to the intrigue and mystique surrounding this tiny part of the human brain.

So what about the holy books? Are they telling us something about the spiritual connection of the pineal gland? So, there is no direct mention of the pineal gland and spirituality in the primary texts of Judaism, Christianity, or Islam. The connection between the pineal gland and spirituality seems to be a product of later interpretations, philosophies, and traditions rather than something found in these religious scriptures.

In some Eastern traditions, such as Hinduism and certain forms of Buddhism, the "third eye" is often associated with spiritual insight, intuition, and enlightenment. In various New Age teachings, the "third eye" is often associated with clairvoyance, spiritual vision, and the ability to perceive subtle energies. It is sometimes linked with the pineal gland, as mentioned earlier.

In these teachings, the third eye is often seen

as something that can be developed or awakened through specific spiritual practices, such as meditation, visualization and chanting. It's connected to a broader understanding of spiritual growth and pursuing higher states of consciousness.

According to some ancient scriptures, it is said that the pineal gland contains all the information about sacred geometry and creation, and it might be considered a gateway to the soul and the divine. These ideas suggest that the gland contains sacred knowledge.

Intriguingly, the pineal gland is reportedly more active during sleep, in darkness and at higher altitudes.

Some have speculated that this might explain why many religious shrines and temples are at higher altitudes.

For instance, it's known that the Prophet Muhammad frequently retreated to Mount Hira, and it was there that he received his first revelation. While there's no concrete evidence linking these practices to the pineal gland's function, the idea does provoke thoughtful consideration and curiosity.

And I believe that through meditation, we can train our pineal gland, enhancing our spirituality activating our intuition and connection to the divine. This might also help us control our minds and overthinking as we connect more with our Third Eye.

Third Eye Meditation: Opening Your Inner Vision

If you want to train your Third Eye, scan this QR Code below and exercise my guided meditation on YouTube.

You might be curious why I haven't discussed topics like the Chakras and Aura until now, especially concerning the third eye chakra. The good news is that the second book will explore the deeper spiritual aspects. But before diving into that, it's essential to understand the principles of the subconscious mind and how they affect our lives. As I mentioned, you can't bypass this subject and connect to your soul without addressing these foundational concepts.

Many people in the modern era may struggle to fully embrace spiritual teachings because they view this mystical information as unscientific. I believe this leads to a disconnection from the Soul and the Divine, which could be why many feel lost and aimless in life. Without a connection to your Soul, understanding the true purpose of life becomes difficult. You might wonder, "What is this true purpose?" In my view, it's about discovering the infinite potential within your human body, living life to the fullest with this wisdom, and creating a magical existence.

And the mystical powers of people whose pineal gland is highly active make it possible for them to be in touch with their divinity.

Our Brain Waves: How Theta Frequencies and Childhood Experiences Shape Our Core Beliefs

Our brain operates with five types of wave frequencies, each associated with different states of consciousness and mental activity. Here's an overview:

1.) Gamma Waves (30-100 Hz): These are the fastest brain waves associated with high-level cognitive functioning, including learning, problem-solving and perception. Gamma waves are often more prominent during intense focus and concentration.

2.) Beta Waves (13-30 Hz): Active during our waking, daily life, Beta waves are present when we're engaged in tasks that require attention, thinking and decision-making. These waves are common during work, conversation and other alert states.

3.) Alpha Waves (8-13 Hz): Alpha waves signify a relaxed and calm state of mind. Often prevalent during meditation or moments of tranquility, these waves represent a bridge between the conscious and subconscious mind, allowing for creativity and introspection.

4.) Theta Waves (4-8 Hz): Theta waves are linked to the state between wakefulness and sleep, often experienced during deep meditation, light sleep or daydreaming. This frequency connects to the subconscious and may facilitate vivid imagery and creative insights.

5.) Delta Waves (0.5-4 Hz): The slowest of the brain wave frequencies, Delta waves are most common during deep, dreamless sleep. They're essential for restorative rest and healing within the body.

Understanding these various brain wave frequencies provides insight into the intricate workings of the mind. By recognizing the different states of consciousness, we can better explore and engage with our mental landscape, potentially even utilizing meditation or biofeedback to influence our brain's activity consciously. Whether for enhancing learning, promoting relaxation, or exploring more profound states of awareness, the science of brain wave frequencies offers a fascinating glimpse into the unseen rhythms of the human brain.

The theta frequency is particularly significant because it is closely connected to the subconscious mind. This state is often more accessible near bedtime and after waking up. During these moments, your subconscious is open and impressionable, absorbing everything you watch, read or engage with.

Because of this heightened sensitivity, you must be mindful of what you expose yourself to during these times. Violent or distressing movies, TV series, or even scrolling through social media can imprint negative emotions or thoughts into your subconscious. Such imprints may influence your emotions, thoughts, or even your life.

Therefore, choosing calming and positive content or activities during these susceptible periods is highly recommended. Embracing peaceful practices, such as reading an uplifting book or meditating before bed, may foster a more harmonious connection with your subconscious mind, enhancing overall well-being.

Let's now look at Theta Frequency's impact on Childhood Development. Children up to six are often in a Theta frequency state, making their subconscious minds highly receptive. This open state allows them to absorb information readily, including learning multiple languages simultaneously and recording everything they perceive. Theta frequency enables children to absorb everything that happens around them, reaching deep into their subconscious minds.

This period is when deep-rooted beliefs begin to form. Children are like sponges, absorbing the belief structures, behaviors and emotions of parents and other influential figures (such as grandparents or kindergarten teachers). They are particularly impressionable and are often unable to differentiate between right and wrong or truth and falsehood. Their innocence and purity mean they tend to accept all information as accurate, regardless of the context or intention.

For example, a parent might jokingly refer to their child as "an ugly duck". While meant in jest, a young child may not understand the humor and could internalize this statement as a genuine belief about themselves. This seemingly harmless comment may plant a seed of self-doubt and dissatisfaction that persists into adolescence and beyond.

A teenager who once heard such a comment may constantly strive to look good or seek validation from others to counteract the belief that they are unattractive.

They may continuously feel dissatisfaction with their appearance, driven by a deeply ingrained, inaccurate belief formed in early childhood.

This example illustrates the profound responsibility that parents and caregivers have in shaping a child's self-perception. Even casual, offhand remarks can have lasting impacts. It emphasizes the importance of communicating with care and conscious intention, recognizing that children's innocence makes them vulnerable to taking even jokes to heart.

For example, if parents consistently argue in front of a child, this conflict may imprint on the child's subconscious. Consequently, the child might grow up associating relationships with fighting or strife.

This underscores the importance of being mindful of what young children are exposed to, even though they might seem unaware. Dismissing children as "not understanding anything" at this age is a mistake. They actively record everything they see and hear, whether positive or negative.

Parents and caregivers should strive to create a nurturing and positive environment during these formative years, recognizing that children unconditionally absorb the attitudes and behaviors of those around them. By doing so, they can help lay the foundation for healthy beliefs, self-esteem and positive attitudes that will serve the child well in the future.

Children's belief patterns are primarily formed between the ages of 0 and 6, and these early beliefs can be deeply ingrained, making them challenging to change in adulthood. So, if you are unaware of these limiting beliefs, they can have a powerful influence on your life.

Take, for example, a child growing up in a household where parents struggle financially, working tirelessly to pay the bills but barely making the end of the month. Such a child may internalize the belief that money is scarce and difficult to obtain. This subconscious belief, formed in early childhood, may persist into adulthood, shaping how the person approaches work and finances. They may find themselves continuously struggling to earn money, mirroring the financial patterns they observed as a child.

In contrast, a child raised in a wealthy family, where financial resources are abundant and money is not a constant concern, may develop a very different set of beliefs about wealth and prosperity. This child's subconscious understanding of money will likely be more positive and relaxed, potentially leading to a more comfortable relationship with finances as they grow up.

These examples illustrate how our early experiences, observed behaviors, and environmental factors shape our core beliefs. These beliefs, once embedded, can act as self-fulfilling prophecies, guiding our actions and decisions in ways that align with our subconscious expectations. It shows the importance of being aware of our beliefs and the potential need to consciously reevaluate and reshape those beliefs if they limit our well-being as adults.

"Change your thoughts, and you change your world."
- Norman Vincent Peale

Bridging the Gap: Merging Neuroscience and Spirituality for Profound Transformation

Understanding the functions of the brain and the subconscious is a critical preliminary step before diving into spiritual practices. Recognizing our neurological makeup's influence and role in our daily lives, belief systems, and overall well-being is essential.

Unfortunately, some spiritual approaches overlook the complex connection between the body, mind, and soul. There might be attempts to engage in spiritual or energy work without a foundational understanding of how our body and subconscious mind operate. This can lead to dissatisfaction, with people complaining that a spiritual session or therapy didn't have the lasting impact they desired.

Think of Wi-Fi, which is present yet invisible to the naked eye. Electromagnetic waves are sent by various devices all around us, even if we can't visually detect them. Similarly, since the subconscious understands only senses (seeing, hearing, smelling, touching and tasting) but not energy, healing the subconscious only with energy is impossible. We can not see, hear, feel, touch or taste energy with our bodies - just like Wi-Fi.

Similarly, if someone were to approach you with a promise of healing a trauma solely through energy work, it may not be enough to reach the subconscious mind. While healing could be occurring on an energetic level, this approach might overlook a crucial component of the healing process. The subconscious mind requires specific methods to be reached and understood.

The limitation here is that our brain isn't inherently designed to perceive or interpret energies in the way spiritual practices often require. Therefore, energy-based interventions alone might not be sufficient for profound personal transformation.

If the goal is to reach significant and lasting change in one's life, it's crucial to first work with the Theta frequency of the brain. Doing so can tap into the subconscious mind, restructure deeply ingrained beliefs and alter neurological activities. This lays a solid foundation to build further spiritual or energetic work.

Allow me to share my journey, a voyage filled with challenges, disappointments and eventual enlightenment. After my divorce, I was determined to change my life and beliefs, leading me to explore numerous healing techniques. From family constellation work to Reiki, from transformational breathwork to regression, I attended countless self-development seminars and more than 50 therapy sessions.

Despite these efforts, I found myself frustrated and disillusioned. The results were short-lived, only lasting a few months at best. Adverse events followed me relentlessly: financial loss, betrayal, heartbreak and workplace bullying. I felt lost and disconnected from the divine, even questioning whether I was destined to be unhappy in this life.

After four years of relentless searching, I yielded only baby steps of progress. But just when I was about to give up, I stumbled upon hypnotherapy, a technique that transformed my life in ways I hadn't thought possible. Money began to flow, I quit my unfulfilling job, and beautiful relationships and opportunities effortlessly made their way into my life. Tears of gratitude replaced the frustration and anger that had once consumed me. Finally, I had found my way.

I share this experience with you not to downgrade other healing methods but to reveal what worked for me. Hypnotherapy was a turning point, providing rapid and profound changes in my life. My six years as a hypnotherapist have allowed me to witness similar transformations in others, sometimes in only few sessions.

Let me outline why Hypnotherapy stands out as one of the most potent techniques for the long-lasting transformation of the subconscious mind. Understanding that hypnosis is recognized and accepted within the psychological and medical communities is essential. Hypnosis works by awakening consciousness by clearing the subconscious mind, making it an exceptional method with a significant and lasting impact. I can attest to its effectiveness based on my personal experience.

Hypnosis has been a transformative force in my life, and I've also witnessed numerous individuals change their lives after undergoing Hypnotherapy sessions with me. However, it's crucial to emphasize that hypnosis should only be conducted by a certified specialist with experience in the field. This ensures that the work is done correctly and effectively.

I intend to share this story to reach out to those who may feel lost, as I once did. Understanding the bigger picture and finding the right approach can make all the difference. Let my journey serve as a testament that anything is possible, that the path to healing is within reach, and that it's never too late to embrace the beautiful life awaiting you.

So, achieving a radical shift in one's life requires a harmonious integration of a scientific understanding of the brain and embracing spiritual principles and practices. The synergy of these two realms can lead to a more holistic and practical approach to personal growth and self-discovery. Ignoring any part of this process could lead to an incomplete healing journey. This is why my sessions are so successful; I put all the ingredients I describe in this book that are necessary for a successful outcome.

Chapter VI

Subconscious & Ancestral Patterns

The Ancestral Echoes: How Our Subconscious Connects Us to Our Past and Shapes Our Present

I've spent some time explaining the subconscious mind, its connection to the theta brain state and its powerful influence over our lives. However, what I've shared so far is merely an introduction. Now, I will dig deeper, as understanding the subconscious is very essential to understand life.

In 2012, when I embarked on my first self-healing session, my teacher emphasized the need to convince my subconscious mind. Despite her repeated mentions, she never thoroughly explained what it meant. Had I comprehended it back then, I believe my transformation would have occurred much faster, sparing me additional years of struggle.

So, let's reflect for a moment: How many times have you heard the term "subconscious"? More importantly, how deeply do you grasp what the subconscious is and how it operates? For me, unraveling the mysteries of the subconscious isn't just an intellectual exercise; it's the key to unlocking life's complexities.

If we understand not only our own behavior but also the behavior of those around us, recognizing that these actions are connected to the subconscious, our perspective will change. We may find it harder to become angry with someone, knowing that their actions are driven by their subconscious rather than their conscious intent.

The subconscious mind plays an essential role in our lives. Imagine if you had to consciously monitor your heartbeat, constantly regulate your breathing, remember every tiny detail, calculate the exact number of times to blink per second and control how quickly your blood should be pumped to various parts of your body. Sounds exhausting, doesn't it? That's where the subconscious comes in. It manages all these underlying mechanisms, from breathing, blood flow, and heartbeat to the entire motor system and everything else happening in the body. The subconscious takes care of these functions automatically, freeing our conscious minds from the burden.

Even while we sleep, our subconscious continues to work, ensuring we breathe and our heart beats. The subconscious mind oversees all the essential functions necessary for our body's survival.

Think of the subconscious as the computer's hard disk, storing all information without filtering it. This leads us to perform many tasks automatically, encompassing physical functions and our behavior patterns. Consider learning to drive a car. At first, you may operate it cautiously, but as you gain experience, driving becomes automatic. Have you ever gotten lost in thoughts at a traffic light, wondering if you proceeded on a red or green signal? That's your subconscious at work.

This automatic operation of the subconscious mind isn't just a curious feature; it has a logical scientific explanation. Acting as an autopilot allows the brain to function more efficiently, quickly, and with less energy consumption. After all, the brain's primary goal is to keep the body alive, and the subconscious mind plays a crucial role in this essential task.

The subconscious mind is thought to contain memories and experiences from our ancestors embedded within our cellular memory (DNA) to aid in our survival. This concept suggests that our subconscious can alert us to dangers similar to those faced by our forebears. If you've ever jumped at an unexpected sound, this reaction might be your subconscious keeping you on guard, echoing ancient survival instincts.

Some theories even attribute common behaviors to these deep-seated memories. For example, why do women often go to the restroom together in public places?

One explanation draws on our Stone Age past when women might have gone in groups to safeguard against potential dangers outdoors. According to the theory, this preference for communal restroom trips has been carried down through generations. Still, it influences women's behavior today, even though the risk of encountering a wild animal in a modern restaurant is nonexistent.

It's a fascinating perspective, linking our present actions to a system that may have protected us thousands of years ago.

So the idea that behaviors such as women going to the restroom together can be traced back to survival strategies from the Stone Age and is a part of a broader field of study known as evolutionary psychology, which attempts to explain modern human behavior through the lens of evolutionary pressures and ancestral experiences. While some scholars propose theories like those mentioned, they are often debated, and empirical evidence may be limited.

Another fascinating example of behavior potentially rooted in our ancestral past is the widespread fear of snakes and spiders. This fear might be explained by the genuine threats that venomous snakes and spiders posed to our ancestors. Developing an instinctual fear of these creatures would have been advantageous for survival, allowing early humans to recognize and avoid potentially deadly encounters quickly. Some researchers believe this instinct has been passed down through generations, manifesting in today's common phobias. While this is just one piece of a complex puzzle, it's a fascinating glimpse into how our past might continue to shape our present-day behaviors and responses.

In summary, becoming aware of subconscious encodings, some of which might have roots in ancestral memories, is crucial, where these hidden beliefs and patterns can shape your life, possibly in negative ways. So, recognizing and addressing these deep-rooted beliefs could lead to positive transformation.

The subconscious mind is incredibly comprehensive, holding potential ancestral memories and recording everything from the moment of conception in the mother's womb. For example, consider a scenario where a mother becomes unintentionally pregnant, and the father asks to terminate the pregnancy. If the mother chooses to have the child despite this, the baby's subconscious might register a deeply ingrained belief of being "unwanted".

From that early stage, the child might unknowingly carry a sense of unworthiness or the feeling of not deserving love throughout life. This underlying belief can manifest as a continuous effort to seek approval and love from others despite not being aware of its origin. It's a powerful illustration of how the subconscious mind works, capturing even the most subtle early experiences and shaping our behavior and attitudes long into adulthood.

*"Children are like wet cement.
Whatever falls on them
makes an impression."*
- Haim Ginott

Unlocking the Power and Complexity of the Subconscious Mind: Navigating Our Internal Landscape of Thoughts and Reactions

I was raised in a middle-class family, living in a small apartment with hard-working parents. They never had the chance to attend university. Money was tight; we weren't starving, but our finances were always constrained.

Years later, when I entered the working world, I found myself trapped in a job that didn't align with my true self. Though I was secure in my position, I was filled with unhappiness, fear and a profound sense of unfulfillment. Sitting in front of a computer eight hours a day, creating PowerPoint presentations and scheduling appointments, felt like soul-crushing torture.

Externally, I put on a brave face, smiling like everything was fine. In reality, nothing was okay. I even switched jobs, hoping for a change, but the dissatisfaction returned.

I questioned my existence each day, feeling trapped in a 40-hour workweek with only 30 days of vacation a year. It felt like a modern form of

slavery, but my fear of financial insecurity held me captive.

"What if I quit my job?" "How will I pay my bills?" These nagging questions from my subconscious kept me trapped in the unfulfilling employment status.

This changed when I began to explore my subconscious and reconnect with my soul and the divine, and things began to shift. This inner work transformed my life, leading me to a place of authentic happiness.

I share this story because I know many of you may be experiencing similar feelings of confinement and fear. I challenge you to ask yourself: If you were free from obligations, fears, and limitations, what would you truly want to do with your life?

It's a question worth exploring, for it may lead you to a life filled with purpose and joy.

With all your knowledge and consciousness, you might wonder why you can't control your subconscious and change your life. The reality is that our subconscious mind guides more than 90% of our lives. But please keep in mind that the figure of 90% is a commonly cited one. Still, it's more of a symbolic number than an empirically proven statistic, which illustrates the power of the subconscious over our lives.

Even with the best intentions, trying to control our subconscious consciously is often fruitless, primarily when we operate from the Beta or Gamma Level of Mind, where we are at a conscious level so that the subconscious is less receptive to our commands.

Remember I wrote above that the subconscious is open at the Theta level, which means you can not be, for example, at the Beta or Gamma Level and Theta Level at the same time, which leads to the conclusion that you can't be connected with your consciousness and subconscious at the same time.

Let me share here a personal experience to make it more clear. Years ago, when I was attending seminars and learning valuable teachings, I was filled with high energy, as if I could move mountains. However, this energy was gone after some weeks, sometimes months, and I reverted to my previous state. Why? Because all the powerful information I had absorbed reached only my conscious mind, not my subconscious.

So, I was still struggling with my limiting beliefs, fears, and procrastination habit. Also, listening to motivational videos that focused solely on "thinking positively" began to frustrate me. I knew that I had to think positively and that I had to elevate my frequency to be able to manifest the things I wanted. But it didn't work out. And this drove me really, really crazy. Now, I know that my subconscious wasn't involved, which was why I failed so many times.

So, how do you realize when your subconscious mind is healing? Trust me; you'll know because your life starts shifting. When that moment arrives, you'll discover you've broken free from the vicious circle that once held you captive. Your life will transform permanently and beautifully, affirming that you've indeed embraced a new, empowering chapter.

The subconscious mind has the remarkable ability to perceive and process a multitude of information simultaneously, far beyond our conscious awareness. While assigning exact figures to this capability is challenging, it's widely recognized that the subconscious operates at a speed and efficiency many times greater than our consciousness. A 2022 study from the University of Cambridge analyzed brain scans and activity data and estimated that, on average, a person has around 6,200 subconscious thoughts per day. This was based on assessing spontaneous fluctuations in brain activity linked to mind-wandering and internal thoughts. Other studies have produced estimates ranging from 12,000 thoughts per day

on the low end to 50,000 on the high end. The variation may be due to differences in how thoughts are defined and measured.

We are dealing with an extraordinary mechanism that allows us to navigate the complexities of our lives without being overwhelmed by the sheer volume of information we encounter.

Let me illustrate this for you. Consider the complexity of attempting to perform a mathematical calculation, sketching an image and identifying a distant sound, all at the exact moment. Consciously focusing on these various tasks simultaneously would be nearly impossible, as your attention would need to be singularly devoted to each one. However, the subconscious mind operates differently. It has the incredible ability to manage all three tasks simultaneously without needing the focused attention our conscious minds would require.

While our conscious mind processes information at approximately 2000 bits per second, our subconscious mind can handle an astounding 4 billion bits per second (Source: often attributed to Stanford University, though the numbers may be more illustrative than empirically proven). This comparison underscores the remarkable difference in the capabilities of the conscious and subconscious minds.

Our subconscious mind records data and experiences throughout our lives, automatically reacting to similar situations to protect us from perceived danger. Consider the example of someone who has experienced a severe car accident at a specific intersection. This traumatic event becomes a deeply ingrained negative memory in the subconscious, influencing future behavior. Anxiety may show up every time this person approaches that intersection or similar intersections. Their heart may begin to beat faster, and they might feel a surge in stress-inducing hormones. Regardless of convenience, they may even choose alternate routes to avoid the intersection altogether. This reaction is not just a fleeting fear; it's an automatic response attached to the subconscious, a protective mechanism shaped by past experiences.

Such automatic reactions are deeply rooted but not set in stone. With careful reflection, understanding, and possibly professional assistance, it is possible to modify these ingrained responses, turning them from hindrances into constructive guides for future behavior.

Understanding Patterns, Overcoming Resistance and Embracing Change: Breaking Free from Self-Sabotage

Let's explore another example to understand how the subconscious mind forms patterns that can influence our lives. Imagine a child who has witnessed a deeply troubling family incident, such as a father cheating on the mother. This experience, coupled with the raw emotion felt at the time, could become a lasting memory in the child's subconscious mind.

As the child grows and matures, this embedded memory might develop into a generalized belief pattern like "all men or women cheat." Though rooted in a single incident, this belief can profoundly shape the person's relationship approach. They may enter every new romantic relationship with an underlying suspicion, a fear of betrayal always lurking in the background.

Even the most genuine and loving partner might be met with doubt and mistrust stemming from that early childhood memory.

Of course, it's important to note that these patterns aren't absolute. People's subconscious minds function in complex and varied ways, creating unique responses to similar experiences. What becomes a guiding belief for one person may have no lasting impact on someone else, even if they've been through a comparable situation.

The critical factor here is awareness. Without it, you risk becoming trapped in a victim role mentality for the rest of your life. Consider the people you know stuck in this mindset, believing they are powerless to change their circumstances. Realize that by engaging with this material, you are taking essential steps towards breaking free from those restrictive patterns. You seek understanding and control over your life's direction, a pursuit that sets you apart from those who feel doomed to be victims. By even reading this book, you are embracing a path of empowerment and self-determination, moving away from a life dictated by past experiences and towards a future you can shape and define.

But why do so many individuals resist change, even when stuck in negativity? Why do they complain about their circumstances without taking steps to improve them? The answer lies in the subconscious mind's natural aversion to change. As I mentioned, the subconscious mind's primary objective is to keep you alive, associating change with risk and uncertainty. Instead, it would imprison you in a known but uncomfortable routine and not allow you to risk the unknown. Change, no matter how potentially beneficial, is seen as a threat. As a result, when you decide to make a change, your subconscious mind may resist fiercely, trying to undermine and sabotage your efforts. Your determination and desire for change become crucial at this juncture, as they will fuel your ability to overcome this inner resistance and move toward a more positive future.

When your desire for change becomes strong enough, it begins to overcome the subconscious

resistance and the subconscious mind starts to relent. However, this is only the beginning of the journey and it's not as simple as flipping a switch. You're essentially running your 10% conscious effort against the 90% subconscious patterns that have guided your life until now. The figures here are symbolic, illustrating the significant challenge you face.

I'm not saying this to discourage you but emphasizing that change, particularly at the subconscious level, is not easy. It requires consistent effort, self-awareness, and a willingness to confront deeply ingrained patterns and beliefs that may have shaped your life for years or even decades.

Is it an unreachable challenge? Absolutely not. It's possible to create profound and lasting change, as I've experienced in my own life. If I could do it, so can you. But it's essential to recognize the depth of the undertaking and approach it with determination and patience. It's a transformative process that doesn't happen overnight, but with persistence, you'll break free from limiting beliefs and open up new possibilities for your future.

Generally, our subconscious mind tends to create illusions that keep us firmly in our comfort zone. It's as if there's a voice whispering in your ear, always ready with an excuse or a doubt: "Why not put it off until later? Do you really need to try this now? What if it doesn't work out? What if all your efforts are for nothing? You're not good enough; don't even attempt it; you'll only fail." These negative thoughts and phrases often surface, acting as barriers that hold you back and lower your motivation.

Many people find themselves trapped in self-sabotage, succumbing to delusions that lead to unhappiness. Instead of reflecting inwardly to find solutions, it's all too common to look for someone to blame. Whether casting blame on oneself, parents, the universe, a boss, or romantic partners, the pattern is the same: there's always someone at fault. Phrases like "I'm in this situation because of what they did to me" or "If I hadn't trusted them, I wouldn't be hurt; now my life is ruined" only hold us back. These thoughts focus on past events without offering any path forward.

The real challenge isn't identifying who is to blame but shifting focus to address and change the existing problem. By moving beyond the blame game and looking for constructive ways to transform the situation, we can begin to heal and grow rather than remain stuck in a cycle of resentment and regret.

Keep in mind that your energy follows your focus. If you concentrate on the negative aspects of life, you will only attract and create more negativity.

Your illusions are, in essence, your own demons. Rather than battling these illusions, it's crucial to recognize them and respond appropriately. Fighting them only drains your energy, distancing you from your true self instead of bringing you closer. If this cycle persists, you may find yourself confined within limitations, never able to realize the life of your dreams.

In essence, if you continually complain about the causes of your problems and why you can't resolve them, you are reinforcing your illusions. Keep in mind that all our thoughts are transmitted to neurons as signals. The more we focus on specific thoughts, the more we strengthen the connections between those neurons, influencing what we attract into our lives.

Rather than complaining about the problems, if you focus calmly on finding solutions, your subconscious mind will work with you to solve the issue. Although much of our brain's activity occurs subconsciously, serving our conscious desires is entirely possible. We are in charge, but often, we don't know how to assert that control, allowing the brain and subconscious mind to dominate. When unresolved emotions are added to this mix, we can find ourselves in a position where we feel trapped and unable to move forward.

Statements like "It's too hard for me to change my life; I can't do this; it's impossible; how will things ever be different?" keep you stuck in a cycle of negativity. Unfortunately, with this mindset, your life will likely remain stagnant as you focus on the obstacles rather than the possibilities. To allow your life to flow and transform more efficiently, shifting your mindset and concentrating on what you can achieve rather than what holds you back is essential.

The Chains of Childhood: Subconscious Patterns and the Search for Love and Acceptance

So let's come back again to the childhood. Remember, everything we experience between the ages of 0-6 is recorded in our subconscious as it is and seriously affects our future. The assertion that 80% of our personality and belief structure is shaped between 0 and 6 is a commonly cited figure and simplifies a more complex issue. This idea stems from the observation that early child-hood is a highly formative pe-riod in human development.

During these early years, the brain is proliferating, and children are learning and absorbing information at an extraordinary rate. They develop attachments, form their first social and emotional bonds, and acquire language and cognitive skills. The experiences and environment during this period can have a lifetime impact on a child's development, potentially shaping aspects of their personality, beliefs and behaviors.

However, human development is a lifelong process, and personality, beliefs and behaviors continue to be shaped and influenced throughout the lifespan. Teenage Years, for instance, is another critical development period, with significant changes in brain structure and function that can also significantly impact personality and behavior.

If you experienced a lack of validation and security during childhood, it might be challenging to take confident steps later in life. Your subconscious mind might constantly seek approval from those around you, influencing your social interactions. Consequently, you might struggle to express yourself freely in essential conversations, holding back out of a feeling of inadequacy. Unconsciously attempting to prove your worth to others can become a draining, lifelong effort. You may often feel exhausted and discontented without fully understanding the root cause of these feelings, unaware that they come from unresolved issues from your past.

Reflecting on my own past, I realize I was completely unaware of my weaknesses. More problematically, I was closed off to feedback, interpreting any constructive criticism as a personal attack. This would send me into a defensive mode, and I constantly blamed others for my struggles rather than taking responsibility for them. I was trapped in the mindset of a perfect victim.

If someone is this closed off to feedback or self-improvement, how can they become aware of their limiting beliefs or identify the root causes of these beliefs within their subconscious? In my extensive experience, after hundreds of sessions, I've found that very few individuals are able to pinpoint the trustworthy source of their suffering. Many of my clients were unaware of where their pain and turmoil originated.

That's why I always emphasize the importance of seeking professional help. When you're caught up in the drama of your life, it's difficult to see the whole picture. You need an outsider's perspective like a film director guides the production from a vantage point separate from the actors on set.

Some people tell me they work on their subconscious minds independently, and while I believe self-work is possible, it's challenging to reach the deep theta level without guidance. Whether through guided meditation or professional hypnotherapy sessions, assistance is often essential to genuinely delve into the subconscious. The subconscious mind is incredibly clever and may trick you into thinking you've resolved an issue when you've barely scratched the surface.

When you reach out to a professional for assistance, they can guide you through past common obstacles, ensuring you transform them. If you attempt to address the issues on your own, it may not lead to the same significant changes you desire. Recognizing this allows you to approach your personal development with a more inform-ed perspective, better preparing you to find the help necessary to grow and make meaningful improvements in your life.

You must recognize that your limiting beliefs extend into all areas of your life, not just personal relationships or financial matters. They can affect interactions with colleagues, supervisors, family, friends, and even strangers. For instance, if you tend to be a people pleaser, putting others' needs ahead of your own, this pattern doesn't just apply to one aspect of your life. Your subconscious mind doesn't differentiate between these relationships. Trying to please everyone means making everyone happy, often at your own expense. Whether it's family, friends, co-workers, or even people you've just met, this need to please can be an all-encompassing and exhausting trait.

So being a people pleaser often comes from a deep-rooted need for approval and acceptance. This need may have developed in early childhood, perhaps in response to conditional love or praise from caregivers that were tied to specific behaviors. Subconsciously, the individual learns that pleasing others leads to validation and affection, creating a pattern that continues into adulthood. The fear of rejection or conflict may further fuel this behavior, as the person may equate disagreement or prioritizing personal needs with being unlikeable or unworthy. Ultimately, the people-pleasing pattern reflects underlying issues with self-esteem and a lack of self-awareness, resulting in a chronic tendency to sacrifice personal needs and desires to meet the expectations of others. Can you imagine the price you pay for your well-being?

I was one of those people pleasers. I was not able to say "No" to people. Even when treated with the utmost disrespect, I lacked the courage to voice my opinions or feelings. The fear of rejection was so powerful that I'd rather be mistreated than risk being turned away. I was utterly blind to this pattern, only recognizing it retrospectively.

After my divorce, I met a man who seemed to be everything I had manifested and fell for him. What I thought was love, I now realize, was more akin to adoration.

During the early stages of our relationship, his lack of responsiveness created a storm of insecurity within me, leading to self-blame and endless questions that revealed my lack of self-esteem.

Thoughts like: "Oh, maybe you wrote something wrong.", "Maybe he doesn't like you and is thinking of quitting.","Maybe I bother him" was exhausting to my mind.

I chased after him, and he knew he had me wrapped around his finger. I allowed this man to have an undue influence over my life, changing my schedule to meet him, putting aside my responsibilities, and ignoring the red flags that were so apparent. Over and over again, he had canceled our plans, leaving me disappointed. Yet I remained ready to meet him whenever he called. His lack of commitment should have been apparent to me, but my emotions blinded me. They took control over me.

I was always ready to meet and spend time with him, although I often felt broke. I was in denial, pitying myself.

Then, after seven months, he ended the relationship, telling me he couldn't give me the attention I needed and that he wasn't ready for a relationship. My world fell apart, and I was overwhelmed with pain as if someone were repeatedly stabbing me. I cried for days, shouting at the universe and asking if they enjoyed the view from there, seeing me suffering for the millionth time. I was consumed by disappointment and felt like

I was dying. I can not tell you the level of my disappointment in words. The pain was so huge. You think you will die in those moments, but you don't. And the suffering is so massive at that moment that you prefer to die than going through this.

I didn't understand what was happening. After numerous therapy sessions and believing my manifestation had worked, how could I have been so misguided? Were all the sessions a lie? I nearly went mad with these questions. I thought I had met my soulmate two years after my divorce, only to discover it was a massive deception.

Now, when I look back, I understand why this happened. As I was hurt by my ex-husband, I was subconsciously attracting men not ready for a relationship to protect myself from getting hurt again. It was a protection mechanism, ensuring I didn't get into a serious relationship that might lead to another marriage. Only with time and reflection have I come to see this pattern as part of my journey toward healing.

"The wound is the place where the light enters you."
- Mevlana (Rumi)

Unlocking Transformation: The Power of Self-Awareness, Motivation and Breaking Limiting Beliefs

I'm sharing these personal examples to high-light the importance of self-awareness. I aim to help you recognize some of the primary limiting beliefs that might be ingrained in your subconscious mind. These beliefs may control your life, just as they once governed mine.

Here are some primary limiting beliefs to be mindful of:

- *"I don't deserve to be loved." (This belief may originate from a childhood where love and attention were lacking.)*
- *"I'm not good enough." (Children constantly criticized or accused of failure might develop this belief.)*
- *"I don't deserve this." (A child raised with frequent punishment may carry this belief into adulthood.)*
- *"Others are more important than me." (A child may adopt this belief if their role models, such as parents, consistently prioritized others over themselves, like a mother who always served others.)*
- *"I must please others to be accepted." (Children who were only praised when*

accommodating others might internalize this belief.)

* *"Success is out of my reach." (Growing up in an environment where achievements were downplayed or dismissed can lead to this restrictive thought pattern.)*

So, if everyone would first work on their limiting beliefs and work with their inner child, the world would be a much better place. Looking around, you can see how many children in adult bodies have not healed their childhood. That's why they may take their greed, frustration, and anger out on others.

If we would try to find out our limiting beliefs and heal our inner child, there would be fewer conflicts and more understanding in all relationships. We can see adults who carry the unhealed wounds of their childhood like they would carry tons of weight on their shoulders without even realizing it. That's why healing one's childhood is of paramount importance.

In my professional sessions, I often delve into a person's childhood, as that's where the root of many negative patterns and vicious cycles can be found. But the journey doesn't stop there; ancestral records also play a part, and it's vital to consider both in comprehensive subliminal studies.

Thankfully, transformation is possible, and I have witnessed countless cases where even a single session has brought about significant changes in a person's life.

Some individuals choose to continue their sessions, finding joy in their progress and desiring to walk further on the path of enlightenment. Others feel content with their progress and decide to stop there. Ultimately, the course of healing depends on an individual's desires and motivation and it's tailored to suit their unique needs and goals.

I would argue that discovering the full potential of your soul and understanding the divine system is unattainable without first healing yourself. How can individuals lacking trust and self-worth reach their true essence? Is it possible for them to discover the boundless potential that lies within?

The principles of willpower and discipline are essential for determining a fundamental change in your life. No matter how many solutions or formulas I provide to improve your situation, without your active effort, progress will remain elusive. Actual change requires a heartfelt desire and commitment, extending beyond just words. While it's common to begin with enthusiasm, followed by a brief shift in perspective and some effort, many people ultimately fall short during the implementation stage. They fall back into old habits, letting the initial motivation fade rather than persevering to make lasting changes.

Two crucial elements spark and reinforce willpower and discipline. These are motivation and the belief that you can change. If you lack the motivation to change, your subconscious mind may lead you to procrastinate and resist transformation. Therefore, the first steps are to raise your awareness, cultivate the belief that you can change and foster a genuine desire for improvement. Finally, you must implement motivation to make these changes, as moving forward is essential.

When these elements align, your life can undergo a radical and positive transformation. However, attempting to change without strong motivation often leads to failure, as the subconscious mind finds ways to resist and sabotage efforts. This can lead to excuses like, "I tried, but it didn't work; maybe I don't have a chance." Your motivation to change must be powerful and genuine. To achieve this, ask yourself, "What drives me to want to change?"

Consider this example: Imagine a house surrounded by water, filled with crocodiles and encircled by electrified wires. Inside one room of the house, there are 10 Dollars. If you and I were standing outside this house and I dared you to risk your life to retrieve the 10 Dollars, you would likely refuse. Why? Because the motivation to obtain that 10 Dollars isn't strong enough to justify the risk.

Now, let's change the scenario. What if, instead of this money, the person you value most in the world was trapped inside that house and you were their only hope for rescue from the crocodiles? In this case, you would likely risk everything to save that person. The difference? Your motivation is now profound and compelling, driven by the desire to protect a loved one.

It's crucial to maintain a high level of motivation consciously at all times. Ask yourself why you want to awaken your soul or achieve your goals. How will your life transform once you reach them? If you can't provide compelling answers to these questions, you might be unable to progress toward change. Instead, you may merely go through the motions and unwittingly repeat the same patterns, stuck in a loop without realizing it.

When I ask people, "What do you truly desire in life? Where do you see yourself in one year or five years from now?" most individuals cannot provide a clear answer. They may speak vaguely about wanting happiness or peace, but perhaps life has much more to offer them than just that.

So, if you are trying to manifest things into your life, you have to know that these four elements need to be fulfilled so that they may come true:

1.) You have to know what you want

2.) You have to know why you want it

3.) You have to believe that you will get it

4.) You have to let it go and don't chase it

Could it be that life is not granting you anything simply because you don't know what you want and especially why? As time passes, you may find that years have passed, and you are still living your life like you did before, feeling profoundly unhappy.

Perhaps, in your dissatisfaction, you might find yourself rebelling against God/Allah or the Universe. You may wonder if karma plays a role in your circumstances. But what if what we refer to as karma is a strategy of your subconscious to rest on it as an excuse instead of changing it? I've had clients who thought they were experiencing misfortunes as a way of paying back some karmic debt. This belief left them with no motivation to change their lives. I've previously written about Destiny as mentioned in holy texts. It's essential to remember that we hold the power of karma in our own hands.

Attempting to heal yourself without sufficient motivation will likely result in your subconscious mind resisting long-term change. You need a resonating reason to wake up with joy and vitality each morning, a reason to exercise, a reason to maintain health, etc. Understanding this is one thing, but putting it into practice is another. You must take massive action to make a real difference in your life. You have to be committed to yourself.

Taking control of your life means being aware of your subconscious mind. However, since your subconscious has been ruling your life, reclaiming this control is like conquering a castle. Just as you would encounter resistance when storming a castle, your subconscious will resist your attempts to dethrone it. But the encouraging news is that you can fully transform your subconscious mind with patience and perseverance. Once this transformation is achieved, it will work in your favor for the long term.

So I want to encourage you to write down your motivation, and then change will be much easier for you. You need the "Why" before the "How" means first getting the Motivation and then taking action.

"It is easy to sit up and take notice; what is difficult is getting up and taking action."
\- Honore de Balzac

Transforming Active Memories: The Key to Breaking Repetitive Patterns and Embracing Emotional Freedom

The subconscious mind does not have a concrete concept of linear time, which means there is no distinct differentiation between past, present and future as our conscious mind does. Everything in the subconscious occurs in the "now". When a memory from the past is triggered, it can feel as vivid and emotional as when the event initially occurred. So when you remember a negative experience from the past, you may feel strong emotions as if you were reliving that moment. Even though the event is not happening in the present, your brain processes the memory as if it were real and current. In this way, you can still be affected by something that happened long ago, possibly without even realizing it. Unfortunately, this tendency to be "stuck" in the past can hold us back from embracing our future.

You might wonder why your subconscious mind often brings up memories, making you relive those emotions. If you frequently recall the past and feel the same emotions as when the event occurred, it's a sign that this memory is "active" within your subconscious. An active memory continues to have power over you and your actions, whereas a passive memory has been neutralized and no longer elicits an emotional response. This also means that when memory gets passive, you will no longer get triggered in the future, and the loop of similar events stops.

For example, let's say someone was betrayed by their partner and felt intense sadness and anger, and if those emotions still arise when they think of the betrayal months or even years later, that is a sign that the memory is still active.

There might also be a lingering fear of betrayal that can shadow subsequent relationships. The subconscious might ask, "What if I'm betrayed again?" Remember what was mentioned earlier: energy follows focus. The more one repeats the potential for betrayal in a relationship, the greater the likelihood of it manifesting. Then, when it happens, we often lament, "I knew it would happen." But in doing so, we forget that our consistent focus might have played a role in its occurrence.

However, if the negative memory becomes passive, you barely remember the situation of the past as if it happened centuries ago but without any emotional charge. You may even find humor in the experience when you look back. Then, you find trust again in the new relationship, knowing that not everyone is betraying you.

This is precisely how I am feeling right now. I can smile about past experiences that once made me cry and feel like dying.

The difference between active and passive memories lies in their emotional impact and the influence they continue to exert on your present life. By neutralizing the emotional charge of memory, you release yourself from its influence, and you don't get triggered anymore by any other events.

To delve deeper into this concept, as I mentioned earlier, nearly 99.9% of our body is composed of energy, and people may carry trapped emotions within their bodies. These emotions are linked to active memories and energies. When you encounter a situation similar to a past event, it may trigger the same emotional response because that energy of the emotion is still present within you.

In my own life, I had huge problems with my father, especially his neglect of me. Throughout my childhood, he acted like I didn't exist for him, never inquiring about my well-being or needs.

We had never had a father-daughter conversation. And believe me, when I say never, I mean it. This neglect continued until I left home at 27, leaving me with deep-seated issues with men, both in relationships and professionally.

This deeply rooted anger towards my father was extended to all men. I got easily angry back then towards my ex-husband. I had a supervisor at work who shouted at me and triggered my anger more, so I cried when I got home. It was a nightmare for years. The negative energies of these emotions were so overpowering that they drew men into my life who would trigger my anger, mirroring my feelings towards my father.

Then, I started working on this specific topic, but healing from these emotional wounds required more than just a single session. I had to work diligently to release the pent-up emotions, but the effort paid off. I now feel liberated and free from those burdens, and I no longer attract the kinds of men who once triggered my anger. Instead, I find myself surrounded by kind and loving individuals.

This transformation illustrates the importance of changing active memories in the subconscious into passive ones. When those emotionally charged memories are neutralized, the repetitive pattern that once ruled my life ends, allowing for positive change and growth.

When you manage to release the energy of the emotion, the associated emotion dissipates for the long term and you can no longer attract similar situations into your life. The energy of the emotion has been released, so there's nothing left to draw those recurring experiences to you. In other words, if you've undergone healing but still find yourself triggered by the same emotions - perhaps to a lesser degree - it's a significant indication that some trapped emotions may still reside in your body. Without completely releasing these energies, you might continue to experience similar emotional reactions. I'll delve into more details later about the connection between the energy of emotion and our heart, as this is another important topic that needs to be understand.

Another significant issue with active memories is that since the subconscious mind doesn't recognize the concept of time, constant negative thinking about a past event can increase the likelihood of attracting similar situations in the future due to the law of attraction. You have to prevent a continued focus on negative scenarios that may be repeated in your mind over and over again.

But why is the mind thinking so much negative? This kind of negative thinking is a protective mechanism from the subconscious. It takes information from the past and uses it to construct possible future scenarios to avoid similar harm. This is where fear and anxiety can arise.

Each time you visualize a potentially harmful outcome, the trapped emotion associated with that memory is activated. It triggers you, even if there was no event in real time but only made up in your mind.

Why does your heart beat faster when you think of a negative thought, even if it's not real? Consider this example: You might imagine a confrontation with a co-worker who always triggers you. You feel angry and agitated even though you are sitting on the couch with your family. Your family members may become confused, not understand why you suddenly seem mad and may think they did something wrong.

Some individuals might feel guilty about this reaction, while others may not even be aware of what just happened. They are merely mentally preparing for the next possible "battle" at work by creating various scenarios in their mind. Later, they might realize that most of these imagined scenarios never materialize.

But the emotions feel very real at the moment because your mind treats the imagined experience as if it were happening. And this overwhelm of emotions may lead to anxiety.

Your subconscious takes the imagined event and the associated feelings and treats them as possible. This can lead, for example, to un-intentionally avoiding or even sabotaging new relationships to prevent the same painful experi-ence from happening again.

And this is valid for each area in life, not only relationships. You may sabotage your business, your health, your friendships, etc. By understanding this behavior of your sub-conscious, you may quickly discover how often you have unknowingly hindered your progress. I hear a lot of people saying, for example, "I want to have a new relationship, but there is no one." This is a typical excuse coming from the sub-conscious because of the reasons mentioned above.

It's essential to remain present and live in the moment. When we do this, we are neither dwelling in the past nor anxious about the future. Remember, our lives are shaped in the space known as "the now". Every thought, action, and decision we make in the present moment lays the groundwork for our future reality. If we continually nourish our minds with negative thoughts, we focus our energy in that direction, effectively shaping our futures. You can liken it to planting seeds; the thoughts we sow in the present are the seeds that will determine the shape of our future.

When you constantly tell yourself, "I hope I don't get ill," what's likely to happen? You might end up feeling unwell. Why? Because you're wiring neural connections associated with illness. So your brain gets your command about getting ill and realizes it. This is a basic example, but the principle can be applied to any thought pattern. Conversely, positive thinking works in the same way. If you imagine in your mind that your meeting will be a success, chances are, it will be.

Fortunately, not every negative thought turns into reality. Otherwise, life would be a continuous struggle for us. It depends more on how much you repeat them over and over again in your mind. Because repetitive negative thoughts are transfered to neurons, at this point, you create your reality, in other words, your destiny, your karma.

You may realize how much I repeated the importance of your thoughts until now. The reason is that I can't highlight it enough.

The subconscious mind cannot evaluate or differentiate between negative and positive thoughts; it simply receives the input we provide. You can compare it to a small child who believes everything that is told without questioning. Just as a child primarily operates in the theta frequency until the age of six, being more in connection with the subconscious, so does our subconscious mind function in a similar childlike manner. It illustrates that we must approach our subconscious as we would a child, accepting and understanding its nature without judgment.

When you dwell on negative thoughts, the subconscious mind doesn't warn you that your

thoughts may be harmful. Instead, it interprets this as a directive, thinking, "My master wants something negative to occur, so I must create it." It then collaborates with the brain, influencing your behavior. As your actions resonate with this negative frequency, you unwittingly draw more negativity into your life. This self-created cycle continues, trapping you in a chain of negative experiences, and you may wonder why bad things keep happening to you.

Whatever thoughts and beliefs you feed your subconscious mind, you'll find they influence what you attract into your life. Suppose you continually find yourself drawing the same types of people or repeatedly facing similar events. In that case, the root cause likely lies in your pattern of thinking and the underlying beliefs that shape it.

*"Watch your thoughts;
they become your words;*

*Watch your words,
they become your actions;*

*Watch your actions,
they become your habits;*

*Watch your habits,
they become your character;*

*Watch your character,
it becomes your destiny."*

- Lao Tzu

Chapter VII

Heart & Emotional Dynamics

The Heart-Brain Connection: Revealing the Emotional Core of Our Consciousness

The subconscious mind places significant emphasis on experiences paired with intense emotions. When an event is deeply emotional, the subconscious records it with greater intensity, potentially leading to a trauma or belief pattern connected to that experience if it is a negative one.

I want to give you an example of this. Do you remember where you were when the news of the 9/11 attacks in New York broke in 2001? Most people remember this vividly. However, if I asked where you were two days before that event, chances are high that you wouldn't remember it clearly. Why this immense contrast in memory? It's primarily due to the emotions tied to the event. Our subconscious mind deeply embeds experiences that are accompanied by strong emotions. In the case of 9/11, the event (which our brain registers) combined with the powerful emotions (which resonate in our heart center) makes it a memory that stands out.

I'll explain the heart-brain relation later, but this is how they collaborate together. Now, let me give another example to show you the importance and role of emotions linked to memories.

Imagine hearing the song that played during your first dance at your wedding years after divorcing that person. You may find yourself overcome with emotion, possibly even moved to tears. This reaction occurs because the song is linked to a profoundly emotional moment of your life - marrying someone you once considered the love of your life. If those feelings haven't been healed, the emotion lingers within you, and you may find yourself crying or struggling to hold back tears every time you hear that particular song.

Or imagine catching a smell of a particular candy scent, and suddenly, you're transported back to your childhood. This happens because that specific aroma is linked to memory and emotion. The brain instantly plays back those memories, much like scenes from a movie.

Now that we've delved into the subconscious mind and its connection to emotions let's shift our

focus to the master of these feelings: our heart.

Through years of research, the HeartMath Institute (founded in 1991) has uncovered a profound connection between the heart and the brain.

They have shown that our heart communicates with our brain in ways that significantly influence our emotions and consciousness. Historically, the medical community viewed the heart as an organ for blood pumping The HeartMath Institute's research has broadened our understanding, highlighting the heart's more complex roles. The HeartMath Institute is known for its research into the physiological mechanisms by which the heart communicates with the brain, impacting consciousness, perceptions, emotions. They have conducted various studies examining the heart-brain connection. So, in this part, I will often refer to this Institute.

The scientific investigation into the heart's functions has been a rich and complex journey for centuries. While it's difficult to pinpoint a specific year that marked the beginning of a modern exploration into the heart's broader roles, significant findings about the heart have emerged over time. Understanding how the heart works is vital for medical knowledge and discovering deeper connections to our essence and emotions. It's a dynamic field of study, continually evolving and contributing to a more holistic view of human health and well-being.

Historically, many have believed that consciousness resides solely in the brain. However, contemporary research has begun challenging this statement, indicating that consciousness may not be confined to just the brain. The brain, body and heart interaction is increasingly recognized as a complex system. Studies by the HeartMath Institute show that the heart might play a crucial role in this process. This view acknowledges a more holistic approach to understanding consciousness, embracing the interconnectedness of the mind, body and emotions.

The concept that the heart has its own "little brain" or "intrinsic cardiac nervous system" has been explored by various researchers, including those at the HeartMath Institute. They have researched the physiological mechanisms by which the heart is a highly sophisticated center for receiving and processing information and that it is not just a blood-pumping organ.

Intriguingly, the heart has its own nervous system, often called the "heart brain," which enables it to learn, remember and make decisions independently of the brain's cerebral cortex. Furthermore, the heart continually sends signals to the brain, influencing our perceptions, how we acquire experiences and how our brain processes emotions. These discoveries expand our understanding of the heart's role beyond its traditional function, revealing it as an essential player in our emotional and cognitive processes.

A mindblowing fact is that the heart's communication with the brain generates electrical activity around 60 times greater than the brain's. This enables it to reach every cell in the body. And what does that mean?

On the one hand, the heart pumps blood and transports oxygen and nutrients to every cell in the body. In this literal sense, the heart indeed "reaches" every cell by nourishing them.

On the other hand, the heart's rhythms and

patterns of electrical activity have been found to influence the brain's functions, particularly in areas related to emotion and decision-making. This connection between the heart and the brain is complex and not entirely understood. Some researchers believe that the heart's electromagnetic field carries information that can influence other body parts, including the brain, affecting our emotions, perceptions, and even our overall health and well-being.

The Heart's Electromagnetic Field: Navigating the Intersection of Emotion and Energy

Some theories, like those proposed by the HeartMath Institute, suggest that positive emotions like love, gratitude and compassion create a coherent and harmonious heart rhythm, positively impacting our physiological state and improving health and well-being.

Negative emotions might create incoherent or erratic heart rhythms, resulting in physiological inefficiencies and stress. The heart's rhythm and associated electromagnetic field could then be seen as a reflection of our emotional state and potentially a factor influencing our overall health. But I will dive into that later. It's essential to note that these ideas are part of ongoing research and might not be universally accepted by the scientific community. More research is needed to understand fully the intricate relationship between the heart, brain, emotions and overall health.

Moreover, according to some scientific measurements, this heart-generated magnetic field is about 5,000 times more potent than the brain's and extends several feet outside the body. This magnetic field is part of our physical being and represents our emotional state, underscoring the heart's profound role in our overall well-being.

Remember, I talked a lot about the emotions trapped in our bodies if we don't heal them.

All the emotions you've felt up to this point are believed to be stored in your heart and its associated magnetic field. Thus, any negative emotions that haven't been addressed or resolved may con-

tinue to linger in your energetic field, potentially influencing your overall well-being.

The heart center is believed to store the emotional weights we gather over our lives, often called trapped emotions. Releasing these emotions can significantly relieve the body and mind, making you feel as light and free as a bird. Issues that once troubled you become inconsequential. Can you imagine the profound lightness that comes with that?

Our heart continually transmits electro-magnetic waves, influencing the entire body. These waves sync with the brain, reflecting our emotional state in various physiological functions. When we experience positive emotions like love, happiness and peace, this harmony is mirrored in our pulse and breathing patterns. Conversely, negative emotions like anger or stress can disrupt this balance, leading to irregular breathing and heartbeat. This imbalance sends negative signals to the brain, potentially impacting our overall function and well-being.

The energy the heart creates in collaboration with the brain is reflected in a person's magnetic field, often called an aura. Depending on the waves you send out, this field may lead them to perceive you as either a positive or negative person. For instance, individuals often described as having "beautiful energy" or as "radiating" positivity likely have a balanced synchronization between their heart and brain.

Occasionally, you may feel uncomfortable or even experience physical discomfort, like a headache, when standing near specific individuals. This reaction might be attributed to the negative energy going out from that person. Understanding this phenomenon can be vital in recognizing how energy influences our interactions and feelings toward others.

When two people meet, their heart centers interact and influence one another through the magnetic fields they emit. It is a kind of energy and information exchange which happens automatically. That means it is a process you can't avoid. Suppose your energy is positive and vibrant, but the other person's energy is fragmented or negative. In that case, your heart may subconsciously feel a resistance, leading you to avaoid to stay in that person's presence.

Unfortunately, there may be times when we sense unsettling energy but choose to remain in that environment. Sometimes, we can't just leave the place because we are together with family members, friends, or business partners. But by doing so, we may unwillingly harm our magnetic field. This occurs when the dominant energy field, whether positive or negative, can influence and alter the other person's magnetic field to align with it.

If your awareness and consciousness are sufficiently elevated, someone with lower energy cannot influence you. In such a scenario, you will either recognize the need to distance yourself from that environment or, if leaving isn't an option, protect yourself from any adverse effects. Unfortunately, those who are not at this level of awareness may become easily exposed to negative energies, continually attracting them into their magnetic fields. I explain more later how that influences us.

You can envision the heart's magnetic field as a conduit that carries and synchronizes information. The emotions originating from the heart are conveyed through this energetic wave, impacting all organs and structures in our body. Think of these energetic waves as a coding system: the transmitted energy transforms into specific patterns within the heart's rhythm and becomes recorded. For instance, when you feel anger, this emotion has a particular wave pattern, and it's logged as a specific template within the heart's rhythm. The exact process occurs for love and other emotions.

In negative emotional states, the heart's rhythmic pattern tends to be uneven, inconsistent, and disordered. Conversely, positive emotions tend to create a balanced, regular and harmonious pattern in the heart's rhythm. These patterns have a corresponding effect on the heart's electromagnetic field. The heart may then respond to similar future events based on these previously recorded patterns, suggesting a memory-like function in how we react emotionally.

Fostering positive emotions in our hearts can increase our productivity and contribute to a healthier body. This optimistic psychological state is often associated with a remarkable reduction in negative inner dialogues and a decreased perception of stress (meaning something that once felt stressful may no longer have that effect). It also promotes emotional balance, clear and focused thinking, enhanced intuition and improved cognitive abilities.

When we learn to maintain balance in our lives, achieving peace and flow in our daily activities becomes more natural. External disturbances are less likely to upset our balance, as our electromagnetic field is resilient and robust.

Here are some ways to protect yourself from negative energies:

1.) Visualize yourself enclosed within a golden or purple orb. This mental barrier can serve as protection against external negative energies.

2.) When you are at home, consider burning sage or other dried herbs and walking around your living space to clear the energies that may cumulate over time. Open a window, allowing the energies to disperse and exit.

3.) During a shower, take a moment to close your eyes and imagine the water washing away all the negative energies from your body and cleansing your emotional state.

4.) Seek the protection of your guardian angel against unwanted energies, always respecting spiritual guidelines and asking for divine consent.

5.) Meditation or mindfulness practices regularly can help you to center yourself and build a natural barrier against negativity.

6.) Wearing or keeping crystals known for their

protective qualities, such as black tourmaline or amethyst, may also serve as an aid in shielding yourself from negative energies.

Magnetic Fields of Interaction: The Heart, Intuition and Navigating Energy in Relationships

Many believe that obvious cues like language, diction, facial expressions and body language define social communication. However, as previously discussed, their magnetic fields interact when two people meet. Let's explore this subject further, as understanding it can significantly enhance our daily lives.

When two people's magnetic fields interact, an energetic communication system is conveyed to our consciousness. It's similar to the expression we use about someone, where we feel either "electrified" by their presence or not attracted at all. These sensations are entirely connected to the influence of electromagnetic fields.

In some scientific experiments, researchers have indicated that information might be transferred between two individuals through their heart's energy fields, even at distances of up to five meters. These studies propose that a person's brain waves can synchronize with the heart rhythm of another person. The more consistent a person's heart rhythm, the more frequent and fluent this synchronization may be between the brain and heart waves with the other party. However, you must be aware that these concepts are still under investigation.

Some studies and organizations, such as those by the HeartMath Institute, have explored the idea that heart and brain waves can become synchronized between individuals. This concept is linked to theories about coherence between the heart and brain and the idea that emotional states can be transmitted between people.

This energy - sharing between individuals is considered a natural ability and is thought to play

a significant role in conveying awareness, empathy and sensitivity from one person to another.

Recent research by organizations like the HeartMath Institute has suggested a connection between the heart and intuitive perceptions. According to this idea, both the heart and the brain might have the ability to tap into a conscious field, receiving and reacting to collective information. This concept might explain why we sometimes feel a sense of foreknowledge about specific events, as expressed in phrases like "I felt this was going to happen; my heart was constricted." Though this energetic information may reach us, we might not always recognize or observe it. By paying more attention to our intuition, we could take preventive measures based on these feelings.

Some research shows a mindblowing possibility: our heart might access intuitive information before our brain does. This idea proposes that the heart's field can connect with a more refined and energetic level of existence, reaching beyond the conventional boundaries of space and time.

For example, during the 2023 earthquake in Turkiye, numerous people, including myself, experienced distress and trouble sleeping in the days leading up to the event. Intriguingly, these feelings were reported by some who were not even living in the area affected by the earthquake, like me, as I was in Germany at that time I felt a profound unease but could not identify the reason for it at the time. Could this phenomenon indicate that our hearts were intuitively aware of the impending emotional impact, recognizing the earthquake as a collective event that would resonate with us?

For me personally, those two weeks after the earthquake were some of the most horrible and unforgettable of my life. It's a remarkable example of how information coupled with intense emotions can imprint a memory deeply into our minds. Fortunately, I've managed to process this memory, so it no longer triggers strong emotions when I reflect on it, as I am doing now. They became passive memories.

Our heart rhythms naturally align with those around us in social settings. This synchronicity tends to elevate our positive energy if we are compatible with the people we encounter. Conversely, when we meet individuals with whom we are not consistent, and if we are not conscious of this phenomenon, our energy may be negatively affected. Recognizing that everyone emits a magnetic field, influencing us in every social interaction and environment, is vital. For instance, some people may feel drained or exhausted after spending time with someone they dislike. This feeling may result from unconsciously syncing with the other person's electromagnetic field, a connection that aligns our energy with theirs.

However, removing negative influences from your life isn't always simple, especially when those affecting your magnetic field and mood are close family members like a partner, parent or sibling. You may find yourself burdened by these relationships, knowing you can't change them unless they choose to change themselves.

You can shield yourself from this negativity by remaining conscious and present during conversations with these individuals. However, aside from close family members where your choices may be limited, it's wise to select the people you allow into your life carefully. They can influence your life positively or negatively. Seek to surround yourself with individuals who are beneficial to you and will contribute positively to your electromagnetic field.

Many individuals find it challenging to distance themselves from those who drain their energy, often due to a fear of loneliness or a pattern of attracting similar people who don't positively contribute to their lives. However, if you're able to heal from toxic relationships and friendships and are prepared to let go, new people with higher vibrations will undoubtedly come into your life to fill those spaces. I experienced it and you will experience it too!

Individuals who are unaware of these dynamics often stick to old energies so tightly that they unwittingly reject new people and opportunities. It's essential to recognize that people in your life you dislike but still tolerate, may serve as mirrors, reflecting aspects of yourself that need healing. In other words, their presence could highlight areas you need to address and heal your wounds.

I once had a client stuck in an unhappy relationship with a narcissistic partner who was disrespectful and abusive. Despite knowing this, she believed she was in love and couldn't live without him. Her lack of self-confidence and self-esteem were at the core of this attachment and these feelings had deep roots in her past.

Her father, too, had been a narcissist and her subconscious was simply mirroring her relationship with him by choosing a similar partner. Since she had never learned what a loving, respectful relationship with a man looked like, she found it normal to endure abuse. She thought she had to bear the situation because it was all she knew. It was only through a process of healing her inner child and

forgiving her father that she was finally able to let go.

By addressing these deep-seated issues, she found the strength to separate from her partner and start living her best life, free from the toxic patterns that had previously held her captive.

As your energy and awareness grow, you may become increasingly uncomfortable around negative individuals. Once you've awakened to a more positive state of being, it becomes challenging to continue associating with those who remain in negativity. This change isn't about arrogance or superiority; it's about recognizing that your connections with these individuals are fading.

Having escaped the role of the victim, you become unwilling to allow such people to drain your newfound energy and positivity.

I had a friend for about seven years and we both had quite a negative mindset during that time. However, when I began attending self-development courses and seminars, I started to grow and change. As my awareness expanded, I realized my friend's constant negativity was draining me. Although we had been close for years, I found her endless complaints about her relationships and her tendency to project her experiences onto me exhausting. Phrases like "Why are women like you and me always unlucky with men?" became a common refrain, taking a toll on me.

It was a constant issue, but I didn't want to be rude, so I simply listened without letting her affect my subconscious mind. However, maintaining this state of alertness around her was indeed a challenge. I tried to be patient, even as I felt drained after our meetings.

My friend was reading about psychology and listening to podcasts, but she wasn't doing the inner work needed to heal her wounds like I did. She remained stuck as I continued improving and thriving, increasingly jealous of my success.

Despite seeing the toxicity in our friendship, I endured the situation for a year, unwilling to abandon a friend in need. But it became clear that she had chosen her path, refusing any advice or help I offered. Finally, I had to prioritize my well-being and end the friendship.

Leaving behind friends who pull you down with negativity is not a selfish act. Instead, it signifies self-awareness and a commitment to personal growth. It's about being at peace with oneself and recognizing that you can be your own best friend. After I let go of that toxic friendship, I found myself surrounded by kind-hearted friends, and I'm grateful for the strength that allowed me to move on.

*"Hardships often prepare
ordinary people for an
extraordinary destiny."*
- C.S. Lewis

The Heart's Odyssey: Embracing Pain, Power and Potential

So, let's wrap up. In our physical world, energy, electrical and magnetic fields play crucial roles in how our bodies function. While the brain has long been considered the body's command center, recent research into heart-brain communication reveals a more complex interaction. Studies have shown that the heart sends signals to the brain, which can influence emotions and cognitive functions. For example, when we feel sad, this emotion may be sensed in our hearts, leading to physical reactions like tears, a drop in energy, or even anger. The connection between the heart and brain shows a dynamic interplay still being explored and understood.

That's why the feelings in our hearts are so essential. Some believe that desires and emotions rooted in the heart can manifest more quickly because the heart's magnetic field is thought to be much stronger than the brain's. This concept underscores the potential power and significance of our heart's desires and emotions.

When you focus on desires from your heart, and your subconscious mind aligns with those wishes by genuinely believing in their attainability, you can manifest anything you want. How conscious have you been of these connections between the body, heart and subconscious mind up to this point?

You can admire the incredible being standing before you when you look at yourself in the mirror. This realization marks the beginning of an expansion in consciousness, where you begin to recognize the magic within yourself. As you become aware of the miniature universe within your body and the limitless potential of your soul, your approach to life transforms, opening the door to experiences that are extraordinary and beyond miraculous. This is where you start to discover the infinity within you.

Why does a divine force permit us to repeatedly undergo the same painful circumstances, whether you name it God, Allah or the Universe? This recurring pattern is often seen as a journey toward healing our innermost wounds. We must revisit these painful moments to face, address and ultimately transform the things that have caused us harm. As mentioned, reaching our true essence and potential is tied to a purification process. In this view, you subconsciously attract similar experiences, and your heart intensifies these emotions to help you recognize and address them. This process is seen as a way to purify and cleanse yourself.

I want to share a deeply personal experience with you as it fits the topic above. After my divorce, I told you before, I attempted a new relationship, but when the guy left me, I realized there were unhealed wounds, and I continued working on my subconscious. Rather than hypnosis, I explored other methods, like family constellation therapy. However, I must admit I felt exhausted. It seemed like an endless cycle of healing, and I wondered where it would end. But with the knowledge I had gained, I was determined to persevere and continue working on myself.

Eventually, my efforts were rewarded by the Universe. While I didn't find my soulmate, I experienced a truly wonderful time. I traveled to Egypt, Cape Town, Istanbul, Antalya, Los Angeles, Dubai, Jerusalem and Tel Aviv within just one year. It felt like a blessing, and I thought I had finally made it. I believed there was nothing left for me to heal. I was pleased and filled with gratitude. During this time, I practiced the 3-6-9 Tesla Method to attract my soulmate. Then, one day, I met him...

That day marked a turning point in my Life. Why? Let me explain. While traveling, I met this extraordinary soul. The way we met was far from coincidental; it seemed the Universe had orchestrated our meeting. I felt drawn to him in a way I'd never experienced before, as if our souls had fused in some magical connection.

This man matched precisely the description I had written in my journal, but there was one detail I hadn't noted, assuming it was understood. It seems the Universe has a sense of humor. You see, he was married and had two boys. And I was not the type to overlook that a man was married. Despite knowing he was married, I couldn't help but fall in love with him; my emotions took control, and I felt compelled to follow my heart.

We met several ti-
mes, sharing beautiful
conversations that lasted
for hours, and in his
company, I experienced
pure love and joy.

Yet internally, I was
consumed with shame,
and he also struggled
with guilt. The attract-
ion between us was
so powerful, like two
magnets drawn to one another, and neither of
us could resist it. What started as a dreamlike
connection soon turned into a nightmare for me.

After spending three intense days together,
I returned to Germany, and the pain in my heart
was unlike anything I had felt before. As with the
previous man, this wasn't just a lesson; something
special resonated deep within my soul. It took me
two months to move on and let go, and the pain was
as intense as I had experienced during my divorce.
To love someone, knowing he was my soulmate
yet unavailable, and to accept that reality was a
profound source of suffering for me.

How can you stop to love someone when
their love has left a deep imprint on you? How can

you command your heart to let go? I cried uncontrollably, feeling as though the Universe had betrayed me again. I couldn't believe that after experiencing such joy and beauty in my life, I faced a setback again.

My greatest challenge was our mutual commitment, which made letting go even more difficult. Yet, I knew I had to because being together was impossible. Although I know nothing is impossible for the Universe, I couldn't build a relationship based on someone else's unhappiness, and divorce was out of the question.

This experience was one of the most significant tests of my life so far. But it also served as a turning point, motivating me to complete and publish this book, quit my job, and start my own business. Because of this experience with him, I purified my heart by releasing all trapped emotions and transforming my limiting beliefs with Hypnotherapy, which rapidly and profoundly changed my life. I discovered my true potential in my healing, psychic and writing abilities. Now I know why the Universe was bringing him into my life. If the pain and suffering hadn't been so intense, I might have continued procrastinating and remained in my 9-to-5 job, perhaps never publishing my book.

Despite the pain, I'm now grateful for everything that happened. Otherwise, you couldn't hold this book in your hands right now.

This story perfectly shows how anything becomes possible by freeing yourself from trapped emotions and limiting beliefs. Until you understand this, the Divine will continue to send you tests. But remember, the Divine's goal is not to make you suffer or be sad; quite the contrary, it is uncomfortable with such situations.

I know this because I'm in contact with the spiritual world as a psychic; believe me, the spirits feel your pain. At least, this is what I experienced.

That's why the Spirits send you messages and signs to assure you that you're not alone. I'll delve into the subject of the spirits in my next book, as this topic is expansive and will require many pages to explore.

As long as we resist the process of self-awareness and emotional healing, we may find that negative experiences and stress increase in our lives. Over time, this can even lead to physical health problems. It's well-known in medicine that psychological factors can contribute to some illnesses, though it would be incorrect to attribute all diseases to emotional causes. While the brain processes these feelings, the heart's signals may guide how emotions are experienced and understood.

Emotions can affect the body and intense emotional stress may manifest in physical symptoms. For instance, emotions like anger might be thought to gather in organs such as the lungs or kidneys, and the emotional burdens we carry may manifest as shoulder pain.

These concepts are not rooted in traditional medical understanding but are considered from a psychological and spiritual viewpoint, inviting us to explore the interconnectedness of our emotions and physical sensations. Realizing this connection between mind and body is essential for overall well-being.

You must realize you are the architect behind your life, not anyone else. While your subconscious mind may seem to govern everything, the fact that you can control it is of enormous significance. You are meant to be the commander of your subconscious mind, but if you fail to take massive action, the subconscious assumes control, effectively becoming your boss. It's time to reclaim your rightful role and switch the dynamics.

"*If you think, 'My life will be upside down,' don't worry. How do you know down is not better than upside?*"
\- Shams Tabrizi

Chapter VIII

Consciousness, Soul & Beyond

Mindful Bridges: Interplay of Soul, Consciousness and Earthly Existence

You may have noticed that I've often referred to the mind, particularly the subconscious mind, but I still need to explain how it connects with the subconscious, consciousness and brain. To truly grasp the interconnected nature of these components, it's essential to understand what the mind is and how it functions within this complex framework. So let's have a look at it now.

In the context of the subconscious and the brain, the mind can be defined as the total collection of conscious and unconscious mental processes. It's like an intricate network that includes thoughts, emotions, memories and beliefs, all working together to shape our perception, behavior and overall life experience.

The conscious mind is the part we actively engage with, the thoughts and feelings we are aware of and can control. It's responsible for logic, decision-making, and deliberate actions. The sub-conscious mind, on the other hand, operates below the surface. It's the repository of automatic responses, deeply ingrained beliefs, and patterns formed over time. This part of the mind influences our actions without us even being aware of it, and it's often where our unexplained fears, preferences and instincts originate.

The brain is the physical hub for the conscious and subconscious mind. It's the biological structure where all these mental processes occur, translating abstract thoughts and emotions into physical reactions and behaviors. The brain communicates with the body, turning our intentions into actions, and it also processes information from our senses, helping us interpret and react to the world around us.

Essentially, the mind is a complex interplay between the conscious and subconscious, all orchestrated by the brain. Understanding this dynamic relationship provides a powerful lens to examine our thoughts, behaviors and emotional responses, opening the door to greater self-awareness and personal growth.

As mentioned, our minds are flooded daily with roughly 50,000 thoughts on the high end. Have you ever stopped to wonder who or what is thinking? This question might lead us into philosophical territory, but let's approach it from a spiritual angle.

In this perspective, our physical body serves as the vessel for our material existence, while our soul embodies our spiritual essence. But where does the mind fit in? Some believe that the mind serves as a bridge connecting the material and spiritual realms. It helps us make sense of our human experience on Earth, anchoring us to this beautiful planet. Without the mind, we might feel uncoupled and disconnected from earthly life.

Meanwhile, our soul fosters our connection to the Divine, God/Allah, grounding His presence here on Earth. The mind balances this equation, working to understand, appreciate and grasp this profound connection. In this view, the mind isn't just a thinking machine; it's a delicate balance that helps us navigate and interpret our earthly existence and spiritual connection.

I want to share an example from my experience during my sessions with various clients. Many of them had a profound spiritual connection to the Divine, yet they were struggling with depression or dissatisfaction. Why did this happen? One of the roots of their suffering lay in a lack of grounding, an inability to understand or connect with their

purpose on Earth. Life felt like a torturous existence for them, and some even expressed a longing to return to what they considered their "real home". This disconnection is often a characteristic of deeply spiritual people who lack a connection to the material world. These highly sensitive Souls have huge trouble grounding themselves, which is why they suffer. It's a complex subject I plan to explore in my second book.

Our mind serves as an essential tool to ground ourselves and enable us to live life to the fullest. What's the point of being highly spiritual if, for example, we cannot generate money to help those in need? Please don't take offense; I intend to offer a new perspective. The world needs you and your unique contributions. One of the biggest misunderstandings within the spiritual community is a negative association with money and wealth. These can be wonderful things when used with good intentions rather than being dismissed or despised. The relationship between the soul, mind and brain is interconnected. Just as the brain takes directions from the heart, the mind receives guidance from the soul and then uses the brain to act on it. For instance, it is your soul that makes you question the purpose of life, and your mind collaborates with the soul to heighten your awareness. This suggests that attempting to silence the mind might not be the most logical approach, as the mind's involvement is essential in our spiritual understanding and growth.

It's the negative thinking, often coming from the subconscious rather than the mind itself, that we should strive to manage and halt, not the mind in its entirety. Like our brain and heart, the mind is a constantly active mechanism and attempting to deactivate its function is like trying to stop our heart from beating.

Wouldn't it be more beneficial to use our minds to enhance our awareness rather than attempting to suppress or fight against it? Unfortunately, our lack of understanding about the nature of the mind has often led us to perceive it as an enemy that separates us from our spirituality and soul. If you view something as an enemy, you'll conflict with it. And being in a struggle with the mind, victory is unlikely.

The real issue isn't the conscious mind but the subconscious mind, which is often the primary barrier to our spiritual connection. Our consciousness becomes distorted due to ingrained beliefs and patterns within the subconscious mind. This distorted state of consciousness distances us from our true selves and hinders our ability to experience life as something miraculous and transcendent.

Many individuals profess to be self-aware or conscious, but a closer look at their lives often reveals a different story. They may continue to struggle with stagnant incomes, broken relationships, or dissatisfaction at work. While they claim to be conscious, what they are experiencing might be better described as distorted consciousness. They have awareness from their perspective, but it's clouded or misdirected, preventing them from making meaningful life changes.

After attending just a few courses, I once counted myself among those who believed they were enlightened. Filled with a newfound sense of wisdom, I eagerly began offering advice to others, thinking, "Look, I've become conscious; allow me to help raise your awareness." Reflecting on those days now, I can't help but laugh at myself. I knew very little, and my subconscious was cleverly sabotaging me. It led me to believe that I had learned all I needed to know from those seminars, convincing me there was no need to explore further. Why? Because my subconscious was determined to keep me within my comfort zone, preventing me from pursuing true wisdom and growth. One of the greatest mistakes many encounter is the belief that they possess complete knowledge or have attained a high level of consciousness.

Reflecting on the past, I now comprehend that scenario, but at the time, it was beyond my grasp. This is merely one illustration of distorted consciousness. We often become trapped in specific beliefs or assumptions, thinking they are absolute truths. Only when the Universe presents us with a challenge or wake-up call can we break free from this limited thinking and ascend toward higher levels of consciousness.

If we quickly recognize our distorted thinking and stop resisting it, the challenges or "tests" we face may lessen in number or become easier to handle. I speak from personal experience. When we hear about these "tests", we often fear them, assuming that they will bring disasters or that the path to enlightenment is filled with pain and trials. In reality, it's quite the opposite. Consider well-prepared students who confidently approach their exams; they pass easily and succeed. Similarly, our spiritual "tests" can be met with grace when we are prepared and aligned with our true selves.

There comes a point where these spiritual "tests" end. This might be because we align ourselves with our true essence and purpose as we grow and evolve spiritually. As a result, what were once considered challenges become natural parts of our journey, integrated into our understanding and way of being. In this state of alignment, external tests are no longer needed to guide or refine us; we're already on the right path.

Overcoming Overthinking: Conscious Understanding of Mind

Returning to the struggle with the mind, overthinking becomes a significant obstacle. Excessive thinking drains your energy, leading to fatigue, stress and a relentless battle. As long as you're consumed by this energy-depleting cycle, moving toward actual existence, positivity and transformation becomes nearly impossible. Ultimately, this path often culminates in anxiety and other challenges hindering your growth.

When you create potential negative future scenarios about what might happen and generate preventive solutions for those possible outcomes, you find yourself in a situation similar to a car attempting to speed up the highway with the handbrake engaged. Rather than battling these thoughts, it becomes crucial to observe them, maintaining an awareness of their presence without becoming entangled in them. You now know that the source of negative thoughts comes from past experiences and your belief patterns.

Imagine you're deeply in love with someone, and your emotions are so intense that you feel almost out of control. At first, the experience is filled with joy and excitement. But after some time, doubt creeps in, and you might start to think, "Will this relationship hurt me? Is there someone else?" These thoughts come from underlying subconscious beliefs about relationships. These ingrained patterns manifest themselves through the mind, and if left unchecked, we can sabotage the beautiful relationship we once cherished. In effect, we become our own worst enemy.

Overthinking appears to come from several interconnected factors:

1.) Subconscious Beliefs and Patterns: People often overthink because of deeply ingrained subconscious beliefs and patterns. These underlying scripts can create fears, anxieties and uncertainties that manifest as overthinking.

2.) Distorted Consciousness: A misalignment or distortion in consciousness may make individuals trapped in endless thought loops. Instead of seeing things clearly, they become lost in scenarios that might never occur, leading to overthinking.

3.) Lack of Alignment with Essence: When not in harmony with one's true essence, the mind can become a battleground, leading to overthinking. The mind might wander into needless complexities without connecting to a more profound sense of purpose or spirituality.

4.) Resistance to Natural Flow: Trying to control or fight the mind instead of observing and understanding its nature can lead to overthinking. When there is resistance to the natural flow of thoughts, it can create a struggle that consumes energy and fosters anxiety.

5.) Influence of Past Experiences: Past relationships or experiences also shape how the mind thinks, leading to overthinking. If the subconscious mind has recorded specific negative patterns, it may replay them, causing a person to overthink current situations based on past fears or failures.

6.) Misunderstanding of the Mind's Role: Viewing the mind as an enemy rather than a bridge between the material and spiritual world can lead to a hostile relationship with it. This misunderstanding might foster overthinking as the individual tries to suppress or fight natural thought processes instead of using them for growth and awareness.

7.) Absence of Grounding in the Present Moment: Overthinking often involves projecting into the future or dwelling on the past, disconnecting from the present moment. Without grounding in the reality of the here and now, the mind can become lost in hypotheticals, leading to overthinking.

In essence, overthinking is a complex phenomenon that might arise from combining these factors. Transforming the subconscious, aligning with one's soul, understanding the mind's true nature, and staying grounded in the present may help alleviate the tendency to overthink and lead to a more balanced and harmonious life. It's essential to approach these aspects holistically, understanding that they are interconnected and mutually influencing. Over-thinking can be a debilitating habit, but several strategies can help people break free from this pattern and lead a more balanced life.

Strategies to decrease Overthinking

1.) Practice Mindfulness: Engaging in mindfulness exercises and meditation will bring your focus back to the present moment, detaching from worries about the past or the future. It cultivates awareness without judgment, allowing thoughts to flow without getting stuck in them.

2.) Recognize Triggers: Understanding what situations or thoughts trigger overthinking can help you develop coping strategies. If specific topics consistently lead to overthinking, proactively manage your response to them.

3.) Set Time Limits: Allowing yourself a specific amount of time to think about a situation and then consciously deciding to move on can prevent you from dwelling on it excessively.

4.) Embrace Uncertainty: Often, over-thinking stems from a need for control or a fear of the unknown. Learning to be comfortable with uncertainty can help reduce the compulsion to overanalyze.

5.) Talk it Out: Sometimes, discussing your thoughts with a friend or a mental health profes-sional can give guidance to gain perspective. Ver-balizing your concerns may help you realize that they may not be as severe as they seem in your head.

6.) Focus on Positive Thoughts: If you are spiraling into negative thoughts, consciously shift your focus to positive aspects or practice gratitude. This redirection can break the cycle of overthinking.

7.) Use a Journal: Writing down your thoughts can support you to understand and manage them. Sometimes, writing things down can make things more transparent and allow you to move on.

8.) Create Actionable Plans: If something is bothering you, create a concrete plan to address it. Breaking it into smaller, manageable tasks can alleviate anxiety and stop overthinking.

9.) Join Activities You Enjoy: Engage in activities you love can be a great distraction and a way to channel your energy positively. Engaging in enjoyable activities can take your mind off troubling thoughts, whether a hobby, exercise or spending time with loved ones.

10.) Look For Professional Help if Needed: If overthinking affects your daily life, don't hesitate to seek professional help. Therapists can provide tailored strategies to help you understand and overcome this pattern.

11.) Understand the Importance of the Subconscious: As discussed earlier, overthinking might be linked to subconscious beliefs and patterns. Delving into this understanding and possibly working on transforming these underlying scripts through therapies like Hypnotherapy can provide a more profound solution.

12.) Implement a Holistic Approach: Consider your overall well-being, including physical health, sleep, and nutrition. Sometimes, overthinking is a symptom of other underlying issues, so taking care of yourself holistically can alleviate this symptom.

Remember, thinking things through is natural, especially when making significant decisions. The goal is not to eliminate thinking but to prevent it from becoming excessive and paralyzing. These strategies offer a path towards a more balanced and harmonious mental state, integrating the understanding of the conscious and subconscious mind and aligning with one's true essence.

"Ignorance is not bliss;
it is oblivion."
- Philip Wylie

Mastering the Subconscious: Unveiling the Power of Thought and Belief

"Who is thinking?" is a profound question that can be explored further. When negative experiences in your subconscious rise to the surface, they can influence your conscious mind, leading you to act out of character or make poor decisions. For instance, the harsh words you might blurt out in a moment of anger, followed by the regret you feel later, can be traced back to these subconscious influences. At that moment, your subconscious mind controls your thoughts and actions like a puppet master.

That's why I strongly encourage you to integrate meditation exercises into your daily routine to help maintain mental clarity.

You don't need to spend much time on this practice every day. Just starting with 10-15 minutes daily can provide significant benefits. Through meditation, your mind will become more settled, and thoughts and illusions will decrease. Just as building muscle in the gym doesn't happen overnight, meditation's effects develop gradually through consistent practice, much like training. It's essential to have patience and not give up prematurely, thinking, "No, I can't do this; my mind won't quiet down."

From this point forward, I hope you'll shift your perspective on your mind, seeing it as a friend rather than an enemy. This change in understanding is a vital factor in uncovering your inner essence. To discover this essence, you must maintain a high level of awareness, and now you recognize that the mind plays a critical role in this process.

When you picked up a book titled "Wake Up Your Soul," you may have expected it to be entirely about spirituality. However, that will be the subject of a forthcoming second book. It has become clear that reaching our authentic essence is challenging without recognizing the insights shared in this current book. Therefore, on this journey, we must first grasp the fundamental nature of our human makeup before we can ascend to higher levels.

If I struggle to forgive those who have broken my heart, fail to transform my ingrained belief patterns, and don't take control of my health, my energy and vibration will inevitably remain low. How can I reach my soul's true potential and connect with the infinite divine in such a state?

One of our life's aims should be to grow and attain a unified consciousness, connecting with God, Allah or the Universe. We are here on Earth to make various experiences and throughout our lives, we gather a mix of both bitter and sweet moments. By leveraging these experiences to our advantage, we can lead a fulfilling life and progress effortlessly on the path to enlightenment.

As someone who has experienced this, I can tell you that when you recognize that nearly everything in your life stems from your thoughts and beliefs, you'll begin to pay more attention to them. With a heightened level of consciousness, particularly one of unity, you'll start to perceive the presence of the divine in everything around you. This sensation can't easily be put into words but must be experienced to understand truly.

If you are experiencing pain or hardship, recognize it as a sign of impending awakening and an invitation from the divine to heal. Instead of fleeing from your pain, seek to confront and understand it. Know that following this path of healing and growth will lead to great blessings. The wisdom of sacred texts supports this idea. **Surah Al-Inshirah 94:5-6** says, "For indeed, with hardship [will be] ease," reminding us that ease follows difficulty. Similarly, the Bible encourages us to see trials as opportunities for growth and perseverance, leading to completeness. The Torah, too, speaks of turning to faith in times of distress, reflecting a universal truth that with hardship comes potential for spiritual growth and transformation.

Recognizing the nature of pain and how it affects us is crucial. However, when deeply wounded, we might forget everything we know and become consumed by the pain. For instance, when I was facing a divorce from my husband, I felt numb and paralyzed, unable to cry or even pray. At moments like these, understanding and acceptance become essential. You must permit yourself to feel the pain and grieve, as this is a necessary part of the process. Attempting to suppress or deny the pain can seriously delay your healing. Instead, embracing your emotions and working through them is the path to recovery.

If you are in a bad mood, it's okay to feel that way. What's crucial, however, is not to let it linger. If the same mood persists after weeks, there's a risk that it might become a habit. At that stage, you must take action to pull yourself together, as the time for mourning has passed, and it's vital to continue on your path, stronger than before. If you feel trapped in sadness, seeking professional help could be a wise step. Remember, nothing in life is permanent; everything passes. But the subconscious mind, always in the present moment, may feel overwhelmed by the pain, as if it will last forever. Recognizing the temporary nature of these feelings is critical to move on in life.

I want to create awareness of one last important topic related to this. During intense grief or pain, people may unconsciously make vows or promises that can have dangerous long-term effects. For example, declaring "I will never fall in love again" after a painful breakup is a significant commitment. Since this vow is often made out of deep emotional pain - a potent form of energy - it can imprint in your magnetic field and subconscious mind until consciously released.

What might be the consequence of such a vow? As time passes and the memory of the pain fades, you may wish to fall in love again yet find yourself unable to do so. The vow once made in anguish can create an unseen barrier, hindering your ability to move forward in love, even long after the original pain has been forgotten.

Your subconscious mind is like a recorder, capturing everything you tell yourself. If you repeatedly say negative things like, "I always have bad luck", or "I'm so stupid," you can make those thoughts a reality in your life. For instance, I used to believe that all the sorrows and heartbreaks I experienced were part of the karma I had to repay. I felt God/Allah continually punished me like I wasn't worthy of love. However, I eventually realized that it wasn't God/Allah doing this to me; I was doing it myself.

By repeatedly thinking and speaking out loud about these negative thoughts, I was bringing them to life. In my situation, I was harboring an ancient, fundamental belief that I didn't deserve love. When people hold onto the idea that they're unworthy of love, they'll encounter numerous challenges, seemingly confirming that underlying belief. So, what is your root belief?

As I began to change my fundamental beliefs, my life underwent a significant and lasting transformation. I've reached a place that surpasses even my dreams, and I'm confident that the journey is ongoing with even greater things in store. I no longer feel the impatience I once did; instead, I'm cherishing every moment and feeling grateful.

**"It's not the Destination,
It's the Journey."
- Ralph Waldo Emerson**

Towards the Infinite: A Closing Reflection

We began this exploration with a glimpse into the greatness of the universe, a spectacle of science and art that both humbles and inspires us. Through the intricacies of quantum physics, we unraveled the connections between the cosmic dance and our very being, discovering a convergence between faith, spirituality and the material world.

We also made a deep dive into religion and tried to understand the common statements of the three holy books. Why was I so obsessed with explaining to you the religious teachings? Maybe, at one point, it even felt like religious propaganda to some of you.

There is a much deeper explanation behind that. On my journey to awareness and my soul, I completed so many seminars about the subconscious mind, spirituality, energy work, etc., and made so many therapies to heal myself. But at one point, something was missing.

I was connected with the universe and the spiritual world, but somehow, I was still not fulfilled. I sometimes even questioned if I was doing right by leaving God/Allah out of the picture as He was unreachable to me. He was like a President, which I never ever could reach. So I thought the universe was something like a representative of God/Allah, so I communicated this way.

I opened myself to a friend of mine and told her that I have the feeling that after all the knowledge and wisdom I got through those seminars, there is a piece of puzzle missing, which I can't find. So I couldn't see the whole picture. And she told me that I needed to learn the wisdom of Islam and reconnect to Allah in a deeper way. More than just believing and praying to a "Stranger" I barely knew. Well, first, when I heard that, I wasn't very excited, to be honest, but it made somehow sense to me. I thought to myself "Let's give it a try." And I signed up for the class that she recommended.

After I joined the class about the mysteries of the Qur'an and Quantum Physics (yes, both in one seminar, which was mind-blowing) for more than 1 year, I finally understood what was missing the whole time. I missed the direct connection to Allah and feeling Him in my tiny heart. No more prayers anymore to someone who was far, far away from me, but on the very inside. Also no more asking from the universe but from the one who created this universe. I even now get goosebumps when I tell you this.

And this is why I explained the religions, the holy books and God/Allah over and over again to you. So that you feel that connection, too. And I hope that I somehow could touch your heart with this.

Your journey through these pages has been a discovery of the world outside and the universe within you. Along the way, we've also examined the holistic view of consciousness, delving into the powerful interplay between the subconscious mind and the synchronicity of the heart and brain. We've sought to understand the importance of emotions, the awareness required in our consumption and the delicate balance needed to awaken our souls. Through my personal stories and reflections, I've shared my path of pain, enlightenment, love and the transformation possible for each of us.

In repetition, the master of skill, we've revisited essential themes, ensuring they take root within your awareness. These repetitions have not merely been words but echoes of truth, resonating with the wisdom of ancient traditions and contemporary insights. Together, we've built a foundation, a launching pad for a more profound journey that awaits you.

As we close this chapter, know that the path doesn't end here. The insights and practices offered in "Wake Up Your Soul" are stepping stones to a greater revelation that transcends the physical and ventures into the purely spiritual dimension. What does it mean to truly connect with our soul, to understand our energy body, to grasp the secret in manifestation, or to attain enlightenment?

The answers to these questions will follow in the next book, where we will explore the structure of our Soul, understand our Aura and Chakras, delve into the meaning of frequencies and vibrations, unravel the mysteries of the spiritual world and enlightenment. Plus of course, much more than that.

In summary, it will be non-scientific and totally spiritual, which will give you the chance to connect to the Spirits and enter their magical world.

Are you ready to take the next step? To delve even deeper into the essence of your being and the divine? The adventure continues and the path ahead is illuminated with the promise of discovery, growth and transcendence. The second part of this exploration awaits, inviting you to a deeper communion with the infinite.

Until then, may the wisdom and practices from this book resonate within you, guiding you toward a life of joy, fulfillment and connection with the very source of existence.

With gratitude and love, may your soul continue to awaken. See you on the next journey...

> **"What you seek
> is seeking you."**
> **- Mevlana (Rumi)**

Bonus

5 Keys that Help Changing Your Life:

1.) Heal Your Inner Child:

Longlasting change starts with healing your childhood first. Without making peace with your inner child, you can't live a fulfilled life.

2.) Transform Your Limiting Beliefs:

After healing your childhood, you should look at your limiting beliefs that you got from either your ancestors, parents or someone else and transform them into empowering beliefs.

3.) Change Your Daily Routine:

Work on your daily habits and change your routine. Start the first hour, for example, without looking at your mobile device after waking up. Do some sports and care for your body to level up your physiologic energy.

4.) Switch to a Positive Mindset:

Positive thoughts will change the quality of your daily life and avoid anxiety and overthinking. You will start attracting positive events into your life. Remember, energy follows your focus.

5.) Change Your Environment:

There is a rule that says that 80% of your good and bad vibes depend on 20% of the people you hang out with. So be mindful of whom you spend time with.

Unlock Your Exclusive Audio Gift: Inner Child Meditation

Dear Reader,

Your journey through the pages of this book is a testament to your commitment to personal growth.

As a token of my appreciation, I'm offering you an exclusive audio download: a guided theta-level meditation designed to help you connect with your inner child to deepen your self-awareness and heal past wounds.

You can repeat it whenever you want to meet your inner child to check up on it.

Scan the QR code below with your smartphone
or tablet to download your audio.

I wish you profound discoveries
on your journey..

"The most beautiful people we have known are those who have known defeat, known suffering, known struggle, known loss, and have found their way out of the depths."
- Elisabeth Kübler-Ross

ABOUT THE AUTHOR

Melissa Kazan

Melissa Kazan, an alumnus of RWTH Aachen University, has been on a profound spiritual and psychological journey since 2012. Her search for enlightenment has been deep and extensive, with an impressive array of 28 certifications in areas such as Hypnotherapy, Mediumship, Trauma Therapy, Remote Viewing, Trance Healing, Transformative Coaching and Sufism.

Melissa's psychic readings are uncannily accurate, with a 99% match rate, and her hypnotherapy sessions have led to life-altering transformations. Through her books, online presence and seminars, she aims to share her profound insights and awaken others to their spiritual potential. Her mission is to enlighten and inspire, one soul at a time.

www.melissa-coaching.com